Old Testament—Series B

by Edward C. Grube

PUBLISHING HOUSE
3558 SOUTH JEFFERSON AVENUE
SAINT LOUIS, MISSOURI 63118-3968

Scripture taken from the Holy Bible, New International Version®. Copyright © 1973, 1978, 1984 by International Bible Society. Used by permission of Zondervan Publishing House. All rights reserved.

The "NIV" and "New International Version" trademarks are registered in the United States Patent and Trademark Office by International Bible Society. Use of either trademark requires the permission of International Bible Society.

Copyright © 1993 Concordia Publishing House 3558 S. Jefferson Avenue, St. Louis, MO 63118-3968 Manufactured in the United States of America

All rights reserved. No part of this publication may be reproduced, stored in a retrieval system, or transmitted, in any form or by any means, electronic, mechanical, photocopying, recording, or otherwise, without the prior written permission of Concordia Publishing House.

Library of Congress Cataloging-in-Publication Data

Grube, Edward C., 1947–
    Object lessons : Old Testament, series B / by Edward C. Grube.
       p.   cm.
    ISBN 0-570-04606-8
    1. Children's sermons. 2. Church year sermons. 3. Object teaching. I. Title.
BV4315.G78   1993
252'.53—dc20   92-42405

---

1 2 3 4 5 6 7 8 9 10   02 01 00 99 98 97 96 95 94 93

**For Renee and teachers everywhere
who shine the Gospel light on children**

Contents

Introduction	6
Made by God (Advent 1)	8
Promised Presents (Advent 2)	10
Best-Dressed Christians (Advent 3)	12
Every Place Is Home (Advent 4)	14
Beautiful Feet (The Nativity)	16
Presents from God (Christmas 1)	18
Yes! (Christmas 2)	20
On a Mission (Epiphany)	22
Hands (The Baptism of Our Lord)	24
Never Too Young (Epiphany 2)	26
Second Chance for Jonah (Epiphany 3)	28
Words in Your Mouth (Epiphany 4)	30
Look on the Bright Side (Epiphany 5)	32
Too Simple? (Epiphany 6)	34
He Doesn't Remember (Epiphany 7)	36
Best Friends (Epiphany 8)	38
Let Me Do It! (Transfiguration)	40
So Sorry (Ash Wednesday)	42
Give Up (Lent 1)	44
Promises Kept (Lent 2)	46
How to Be Happy (Lent 3)	48
Where to Look (Lent 4)	50
Old and New (Lent 5)	52
No Big Deal (Palm Sunday)	54
Tears of Joy (Easter)	56
Regularly Refreshed (Easter 2)	58
Nothing Better (Easter 3)	60
Always a Winner (Easter 4)	62
Welcome Words (Easter 5)	64
Evidence (Easter 6)	66
What's Inside? (Easter 7)	68
Bubble and Fizz (Pentecost)	70
Three Names in One (Holy Trinity)	72

Take a Rest (Pentecost 2)	74
Cover-up (Pentecost 3)	76
Starting Over (Pentecost 4)	78
Silly Questions (Pentecost 5)	80
God's Guarantee (Pentecost 6)	82
A Message for Sinners (Pentecost 7)	84
You Have a Call (Pentecost 8)	86
The Shepherd's Umbrella (Pentecost 9)	88
Knowing God (Pentecost 10)	90
Every Day (Pentecost 11)	92
Bread and Water (Pentecost 12)	94
Y's Children (Pentecost 13)	96
Choices (Pentecost 14)	98
Always Near (Pentecost 15)	100
Back to Normal (Pentecost 16)	102
He Did It (Pentecost 17)	104
From Beginning to End (Pentecost 18)	106
Help! (Pentecost 19)	108
Partners (Pentecost 20)	110
God Is with You (Pentecost 21)	112
Lots and Lots (Pentecost 22)	114
Lost and Found (Pentecost 23)	116
Remember (Pentecost 24)	118
Filled Up (Pentecost 25)	120
Shining Christian (Third Last Sunday in the Church Year)	122
God's Court (Second Last Sunday in the Church Year)	124
Celebrate! (Sunday of the Fulfillment)	126
Scripture Index	128

Introduction

The heart of any sermon for children is the Gospel. Full appreciation of the Gospel requires children to know why they need this gift of grace. Each object lesson includes a Gospel nugget that proclaims God's acts. Children will hear much about God's love and forgiveness. They will also be challenged to live and act in response to the Gospel.

Each message in this book speaks to children from 5 to 8 years old. But don't neglect the 88-year-old in your congregation. Older people show physical signs of attentiveness during children's messages. They appreciate the Gospel simply stated, too. Speak your children's message loud enough for all to hear. Use a microphone if one is available. Several messages in this book encourage participation by the congregation.

Deliver messages in a conversational tone; however, a flair for the dramatic will hold the children's attention. (Be bold!) Don't avoid the modest attempts at humor in some of the messages; they are not irreverent.

Many of the messages include questions to encourage the children's active participation. Appeal to their curiosity, and always expect the unexpected. Some children may be shy and silent if they don't know you. Capitalize on the more uninhibited behavior of bolder children.

Most messages directly relate to the Series B Old Testament Bible readings. If your congregation is not using Series B right now, you may need to make some adjustments. The objects suggested for each presentation should be easily available at home or in the church office. Occasionally, a message suggests that you duplicate a simple item for the children to use or take home.

Practice reading messages out loud. What sounds good when we talk silently to ourselves might not come across the same way when spoken aloud. Some of the messages also require manipulation of the objects. It's a good idea to practice so you can remain comfortable and natural throughout the presentation. Pages of this book are "reader friendly" so you can photocopy your presentation if you desire to read it directly.

Feel free to adjust and modify the messages to fit your unique situation and personality. Several messages invite you to ad lib, but don't wait for an invitation. Spin off the ideas on these pages with your own ideas. Only one request: avoid the temptation to moralize. Each object lesson is intentionally short on "what you should do" advice for children. Children do need to respond to the Gospel, but moralizing is unlikely to produce changes in the heart. Only the pure, free Gospel can do that!

May God bless your message.

Made by God

ADVENT 1: Is. 63:16b–17; 64:1–8; 1 Cor. 1:3–9; Mark 13:33–37 or Mark 11:1–10

Text. Yet, O LORD You are our Father. We are the clay, You are the potter; we are all the work of Your hand. *Is. 64:8*

Teaching aid. A shirt with the size and trademark tags intact. Also, small slips of paper similar in size to trademark or "size" tags found inside clothing. Write "Made by God" on each slip. Provide one slip for each participating child.

Gospel nugget. God made us His children by giving us faith in Jesus as our Savior.

You look very good today. (*Comment on specific items worn by children.*) Did any of you make your own clothing? What might happen if you made your own shirts or slacks or dresses? Your shirts could end up with a mess of armholes where buttonholes should be, or your slacks or dresses might be too small or too big.

I bought some new shirts (blouses, sweaters, etc.) I wear size (*insert your clothing size*), but I didn't know how to find my size at the store. The clerk explained how I could find the right shirt. She said to look for a tag with the number (_____) on it (*show shirt tag*). After I found the right size, I wanted to be sure that I bought a well-made shirt. The clerk told me to find a shirt with this name on it (*show trademark tag and say the name*). Now I'm sure I have a good shirt because it was made by (*mention trade name*).

The most important thing about clothing is not the size or the maker, but the person wearing it. You probably know that God loves you very much. God says you are His very own child. Do you know why? I can think of two reasons.

First, God made you. Of course, He used your mom and dad to give you life. And now God cares for you through your family.

Second, God made you a Christian. He did this by Himself. Listen to this Bible passage from the Old Testament (*read text*). Those words mean He formed and shaped you into His child. He gave you the Holy Spirit so you could know that Jesus loves you. If you had a tag, it would say (*show tag*) "Made by God."

Since God made you a Christian, you are very well made. How do I know? Well, allow me to ask three questions. (*Encourage responses.*)

1. Do you love Jesus? I believe everyone said, "Yes."

2. Why do you love Jesus? You love Jesus because God gave us Jesus as the first Christmas present. Later, Jesus died for our sins and rose from the dead. Someday, we'll join Jesus in heaven.

3. Do you really believe that Jesus loves you? You do? That's wonderful. You believe in Jesus because God gave you faith. Without faith you wouldn't—you couldn't—believe that Jesus took away your sins. Excuse me a moment, while I ask the congregation, "Congregation, isn't it wonderful that the Holy Spirit brought these children to faith?" Let's give God a hand (*lead the clapping*).

(*Distribute "Made by God" tags.*) I'm giving each of you a tag that says "Made by God." You are very special! Jesus died for you. He thinks of you all the time and knows that God put (*if possible, name all children present*) on earth for His glory. He knows that you'll be with Him someday in heaven, too. You were made by God.

Prayer. Thank You, God, for making me. Keep me Your own child by making my faith stronger every day. Thank You even more for sending the baby Jesus into the world. When we celebrate Christmas this year, remind us that we couldn't be Christians without Christ. We pray in Jesus' name. Amen.

Promised Presents

ADVENT 2: Is. 40:1–11; 2 Peter 3:8–14; Mark 1:1–8

Text. And the glory of the Lord will be revealed, and all mankind together will see it. For the mouth of the Lord has spoken. *Is. 40:5*

Teaching aid. A gift-wrapped box.

Gospel nugget. God revealed His long-promised Gift with the birth of Jesus Christ, the Savior.

I found this in the closet (*show gift box*). What might be in a box this size and shape? (*Invite children to guess.*) My (*name family member such as wife, son, etc.*) promised to get me something very special this Christmas—something I've always wanted. I hope it's in this box, but I must wait until Christmas to find out. Christmas is only a couple of weeks away, but it seems a long time to wait for a special gift. I'll put the box over here (*off to the side but in view*). Seeing it will help me look forward to Christmas.

God promised the people long ago that someday they would receive the best present ever. God used prophets like Isaiah to remind people of His fantastic promise (*read text*). The people liked God's promise, and waiting for the Savior actually made them happy.

How does Jesus make you happy? He makes me happy when I think that He loved me so much that He died for my sins. I'm so happy that I want to sing Christmas songs all year.

Jesus makes us strong, too. And do we need His strength! We are sinners. That means that we do wrong things every day. We are sinners even on our best days. All people are sinners.

Have you ever heard the song "Santa Claus is Coming to

Town"? It tells you to be careful—no pouting or crying. Why? Santa Claus won't bring any presents if you act badly. That's scary. The song says that you will get presents only if you're very good. But God gave us Jesus because we can't be good enough to be His children by ourselves. He makes us strong so we can fight the devil and evil temptations. And when we do wrong, God forgives us.

Have you ever received a gift that you could hardly wait to show somebody? Telling others about Jesus is like showing our favorite Christmas present to others. This is a great time of year to tell other people how much Jesus loves them. Sunday school classes are getting ready for the children's Christmas service. Your singing and speaking parts will tell the story of Jesus in a very nice way. Perhaps you could invite a friend or neighbor who doesn't know Jesus to come for the service.

Jesus is a gift that never wears out. We can give Him to everyone we know, and He will still be with us. He always has time to listen to our prayers. He never gets tired of forgiving us. And He will come again to take all His people to heaven.

Prayer. Dear Jesus, we are happy that God gave You to us on that first Christmas long ago. We praise You for promising to come again, and we are eager to meet You face to face. While we wait for you to come back, help us share the good news of Christmas in what we say and in the way that we live each day. Amen.

Best-Dressed Christians

ADVENT 3: Is. 61:1–3, 10–11; 1 Thess. 5:16–24; John 1:6–8, 19–28

Text. I delight greatly in the LORD my soul rejoices in my God. For He has clothed me with garments of salvation and arrayed me in a robe of righteousness, as a bridegroom adorns his head like a priest, and as a bride adorns herself with her jewels. *Is. 61:10*

Teaching aid. Boots or work shoes, shorts, dress shoes, sleepwear, clerical robe or collar; wedding picture (if presenter is single, wedding picture of a close relative or friend). Carry items in a briefcase, small piece of luggage, or paper sack.

Gospel nugget. Jesus makes sinners righteous in God's sight.

Today's Bible reading from Isaiah says that God has dressed us in some special clothes. How many of you have any garments of salvation or robes of righteousness hanging in your closet? You can't buy them at any store. We'll talk more about those garments and robes later.

First, let's play a game with the clothing I brought today. I'll show you a piece of clothing, and you tell me when I would wear it. *(Show boots or work shoes.)* When would I wear these? *(Encourage responses after each question.)*

(Show shorts.) When would be a good time to wear these?

(Show shoes.) Here's one of my favorite dress shoes. When do you think I would wear it?

(Show sleepwear.) When am I most likely to wear these?

(*Show a robe or a clerical collar.*) What is this? It's called a
_____ . Pastors wear these when they lead worship.

(*Show wedding picture.*) Here is a picture of my (spouse) and me dressed in some very special clothing. Why did we wear these clothes? Wedding dresses and tuxedos make the bride and groom look special on the day they get married.

Well now, let's talk about garments of salvation and robes of righteousness. Garment is another word for a piece of clothing. I could call this _____ that I'm wearing a garment. Where do you get a garment of salvation? Listen to Isaiah (*read text*). The Lord gives us garments of salvation. How about robes of righteousness? Nobody can give us robes of righteousness and garments of salvation except God. Do you know who bought those robes and garments for us? Jesus did. He paid for them with His perfect life and with His death on the cross for our sins.

You can't see a robe of righteousness, as you can socks or sweaters. So how do you know if you are wearing a robe of righteousness? Christians have them on all the time. Jesus gave you one when you became a Christian.

Be sure to wear yours all the time. Without it, God would see your sins. He would be angry about your sin and punish you. Scary, isn't it? But our clothes from Jesus cover all our sins. When you wear the robe Jesus gave you, God sees you as perfect.

Prayer. Dear Lord Jesus, we thank You for making us look good to God. Always keep us well-dressed in our very own robes of righteousness, and give Your garments of salvation to everyone else in the world, too. We pray in Your most holy name. Amen.

Every Place Is Home

ADVENT 4: 2 Sam. 7:(1–7) 8–11, 16; Rom. 16:25–27; Luke 1:26–38

Text. The LORD declares to you that the LORD Himself will establish a house for you. Your house and your kingdom will endure forever before me; your throne will be established forever. *2 Sam. 7:11, 16*

Teaching aid. Picture of a tent or camper (RV). See catalogs, magazines, or newspaper ads.

Gospel nugget. God through Jesus gives us an everlasting home.

Look at this picture of a special kind of house. What would you call this kind of home? A tent (or recreational vehicle) might be a neat place to live. In what ways might it be a good home? (*Encourage responses.*) It would keep you dry if it rained, and it could also protect you from the hot sun. If you got tired of living in one place, you could easily move your tent somewhere else.

Why might a tent not be such a neat place to live? (*Encourage responses.*) Perhaps it would blow over during a storm, and it might not keep you very warm in cold weather. There isn't much room inside a tent either, so it might not make the best home if you had to live in it for many days.

The people of Israel used a tent for God's home, but King David thought that God needed a better house. Perhaps he said something like this: "God, You have been so good to me and my people. It's a shame that the only house we have for You is a tent. Oh, it was a good home while our people were traveling around the wilderness. But things are different now, and we aren't moving around so much. I'm only a king, and I live in a beautiful palace! I'd like to build a fancy new house for You, Lord."

But God didn't want a palace or any other kind of fancy building just then. Instead, no matter what kind of house God had, He promised that He would live with David. In fact, God promised to live with every person who believes in Him. He lives with us wherever we go. God loves us as much as He loved David and the children of Israel.

If you moved to the top of a mountain or to an island, God's house would be right there with you. If you lived in a hot desert or at the North Pole, God's home would be with you there, too. Listen to what the Bible says about God's house.

"Don't you know that you yourselves are God's temple and that God's Spirit lives in you (1 Cor. 3:16)?" You are God's house! God not only made you, but He also lives in you. That's very good news. God loves you very much.

Perhaps you can tell your friends that Jesus wants to live in every person, not just a few. Invite them to church and Sunday school, so they can believe in Jesus and be God's temples.

Maybe the greatest thing about having God living in you is that no one can ever wreck His house. God will live in you even after you die. Then He will take you to His wonderful home in heaven to be with Abraham, King David, the people in your family, and every believer in Jesus. We will live with God in the best home ever!

Prayer. Dear Lord, thank You for living in us. Make us good temples for You. Work in us to serve You and other people. In Jesus' name we pray. Amen.

Beautiful Feet

THE NATIVITY: Is. 52:7–10; Heb. 1:1–9; John 1:1–14

Text. How beautiful on the mountains are the feet of those who bring good news, who proclaim peace, who bring good tidings, who proclaim salvation, who say to Zion, "Your God reigns!" Is. 52:7

Teaching aid. The feet of the gathered children.

Gospel nugget. God sends the good news of salvation through His word and through messengers who proclaim His word.

Everybody stick your feet out. Wow! What beauties! Look. Here are some long feet, and some short ones. Some are narrow, others wide. What a fine collection of beautiful feet.

In today's Bible reading Isaiah tells about beautiful feet running through the mountains. Those feet belonged to messengers who were like TV news reporters, racing from battlefields to tell the king good news. The battle was over, and the people could look forward to peace. I imagine people danced with joy.

Since it's Christmas, let's talk about some other feet, about shepherds' feet. An angel surprised the shepherds of Bethlehem with wonderful news. What was that news? The angel said, "I bring you good news of great joy that will be for all the people. Today in the town of David a Savior has been born to you; He is Christ the Lord" (Luke 2:10–11). The shepherds happily raced off to see this good news for themselves. Their feet then carried them to their friends with exciting news about baby Jesus.

What other people came to see Jesus? The Wise Men traveled many miles to see the new Savior. Even though camels' feet did much of the walking, the trip must have been long and tiring.

After they gave Jesus some gifts, they were off again. What do you suppose those Wise Men did when they got back home? I'm sure they told others about Jesus, a new King who would do wonderful things for His people.

After Jesus grew up, His dusty, aching feet dragged Him to the place where He died for our sins. And on Easter morning several people saw the nail-scarred feet of Jesus, who was now very much alive again. For a time, Jesus walked among people to show them He was alive. He told them the good news that even though they died, they could live forever, too. Finally, Jesus went to get heaven ready for us. As He floated up through the clouds, maybe the last things His disciples saw were the bottoms of Jesus' feet.

Wow! You probably never thought so much about feet in church before. Now let's talk about your beautiful feet. Like the angels, you have some great Christmas news. You are God's messenger! Shout, "Merry Christmas! Jesus was born for you and me. He died to take away our sins, and He went to heaven. Someday He will come back for us." Stand up on your beautiful feet. Practice saying your best "Merry Christmas" a few times. Now walk over to someone sitting here in the congregation, shake hands and say, "Merry Christmas." (*Demonstrate your instructions. After children have completed the greeting, dismiss them to their parents.*)

Presents from God

CHRISTMAS 1: Is. 45:22–25; Col. 3:12–17; Luke 2:25–40

Text. Turn to me and be saved, all you ends of the earth; for I am God, and there is no other. But in the LORD all the descendants of Israel will be found righteous and will exult. *Is. 45:22, 25*

Teaching aid. A blank baptismal certificate.

Gospel nugget. God invites all people to be His righteous children through Jesus Christ.

Whose child are you? Would I be correct in saying that you belong to your parents? All children begin with a mom and a dad. Sometimes children get adopted by a new mom and dad. Together they make a real family.

In a way, all of us are adopted. Listen to this Bible verse to find out who adopted you. "The Spirit Himself testifies with our spirit that we are God's children" (Rom. 8:16). God made you His children even though you also have regular parents. To become part of God's family, you are baptized. Then the pastor fills out a piece of paper like this (*show baptismal certificate*)—a baptismal certificate. It says God adopted you as His child. Many of you are already baptized, but some of you may still be waiting for that great day.

When God adopted you in Baptism, He gave you some very special gifts. First, a birthday present. Like all the best gifts, you didn't do anything to deserve it. God's first present for you is faith in Jesus. Being baptized is like having a second birthday.

When God adopted you, He also gave you a Christmas present. He gave you a baby Brother. His name is Jesus. And what a Brother He is! He takes the blame for everything you ever do wrong. He never gets tired of being kind to you. And Brother Jesus always has time to listen when you talk to Him.

A third present from God is an inheritance. An inheritance is a big gift, like a house or some money, that once belonged to someone else in your family. That person, maybe your grandmother or your uncle, said, "When I die, I want you to get my house or the extra money I earned." When God adopted us, He promised we will inherit a home in heaven.

Our Brother Jesus is in heaven right now getting our house ready. We will share our inheritance in heaven with famous brothers and sisters from Bible times like Abraham, David, Ruth and Esther. We'll live together forever. We'll laugh a lot and completely enjoy our new lives with Jesus. The best thing about inheriting heaven is that we'll always be with God. We'll be able to talk to each other, and we'll never worry about doing something wrong because we'll be perfect. Heaven is ours because God gives it to us. Free! Let's thank God for these gifts.

Prayer. Dear God, thank You for loving us so much. Thank You for adopting us and giving to us birthday, Christmas, and Easter presents. Thank You also for giving us the inheritance of life forever with You in heaven. Amen.

Yes!

CHRISTMAS 2: Is. 61:10–62:3; Eph. 1:3–6, 15–18; John 1:1–18

Text. For Zion's sake I will not keep silent, for Jerusalem's sake I will not remain quiet, till her righteousness shines out like the dawn, her salvation like a blazing torch. The nations will see your righteousness, and all kings your glory; you will be called by a new name that the mouth of the LORD will bestow. *Is. 62: 1, 2*

Teaching aid. Sealed envelope with scripted message inside (as indicated below). Print "Important" on outside of envelope. Also a note card and pencil for recording gifts from God.

Gospel nugget. God's gift of salvation is the best among the many gifts He gives.

(*Show children the envelope.*) I just received this envelope marked "Important." When something is important, that means I should look at it first. I'm so excited! I think I'll open it right now. Wow! It says, "You're a winner! You have been selected to receive either a new sports car, a two-week vacation on a tropical island, or a genuine stuffed animal." This is my lucky day. After church, I think I'll call some of my friends, and tell them the good news.

Did you ever get some exciting news that you just couldn't wait to tell someone else? What was your news? (*Encourage responses.*)

In today's Bible reading Isaiah says he has such good news that he will not keep still. Everyone should hear it. So should we. Let's make a list of God's gifts to us. We know that God gave us Jesus on the first Christmas. Do you know that Jesus loves you very much? Do you believe that He forgives your sins? If you know that, raise your hand. Look at all those hands. Along with Jesus, God gave every one of you the gift of faith to believe that Jesus is your loving Savior.

So far we have faith and Christmas on our list of gifts from God. What else can we write down? Let's remember why God gave us faith and Christmas. We had one very important need—the need for someone instead of us to get punished for our sins. Jesus was that someone.

How did He pay for our sins? Yes, He died for our sins. And then He rose from the dead on Easter. The Bible tells us that we will rise and go to heaven after we die, too. What a splendid present!

Those are the most important gifts that God gave each of His people: Jesus, faith, forgiveness, and eternal life. Can you name others? I'll keep a list. (*Repeat each suggestion as you record it.*)

One way to thank and praise God is by praying. How do most prayers end? We normally say, "Amen." Today, instead, let's say, "Yes!" (*Say yes very emphatically.*) We are agreeing that God hears our prayers and that He'll do what's best for us. After I read each thing on our thank-You list, I'd like you (and the whole congregation) to say, "Yes!" Ready?

Thank You, God, for giving us the Savior at Christmas.
"Yes!"

(*Continue prayer list with all items suggested for praising God.*)

On a Mission

EPIPHANY: Is. 60:1–6; Eph. 3:2–12; Matt. 2:1–12

Text. Arise, shine, for your light has come, and the glory of the LORD rises upon you. See, darkness covers the earth and thick darkness is over the peoples, but the LORD rises upon you and His glory appears over you. Nations will come to your light, and kings to the brightness of your dawn. *Is. 60:1–3*

Teaching aid. A star ornament like those found atop Christmas trees. Optional: a modern globe.

Gospel nugget. The Lord's grace pierces the darkness in which unbelievers live.

Many people were looking for help at the time Jesus was born. At first, they didn't know about their Savior, but God led them to see Jesus. The Wise Men, or Magi, didn't know the Savior. But off in the distance they saw a light in the sky. It wasn't just any light. It was a special sign from God, a star (*hold star high*). Somehow those Magi knew that they should go where that star was pointing. They traveled many days before finally reaching Jesus. They were so happy to find the Savior. They were even happier to know that the Savior loved them.

Many people still do not know that Jesus loves them. Some of those people live nearby, right here in our own town or state. Others live many miles away. People who don't know Jesus often feel as if they are wandering outside on the darkest of nights. Maybe they feel lonely, afraid, or lost. They need to see Jesus' light.

You and I can be Jesus' light for them. How? Here's a clue (*fold hands*). Yes, we can pray that all people find out about the Savior. We can pray for missionaries, special pastors, and teachers who bring news about Jesus to people who haven't heard about Him. We have missionaries teaching in places like New Guinea out in the Pacific Ocean, South America, Africa, and India (*indicate locations on globe*). They baptize men, women, and children and tell them about Jesus in whatever language they speak. Let's pray for our missionaries and the people they teach.

We pray: Lord Jesus, we know You are called the Light of the world. Shine Your love on all missionaries who share good news about You with people in faraway places. Let the people see Your light, and give them faith. We look forward to meeting You and all Your people in heaven. Amen.

You and I can also be missionaries to people we live, play and go to school with. How? I think you might already know how.

Pretend I'm someone about your age. One day I say to you, "I don't feel very happy today. I'm afraid I don't have any friends. Kids are calling me names. My sister won't play because she got really mad at me. Even my dog puts down his tail and walks the other way."

What might you say to me if I were feeling so bad? (*Encourage children to respond.*) Knowing that Jesus' loves you, especially when you're feeling unloved, helps a lot. Jesus loves you even if you feel like nobody else loves you. If you told me that, you would be a missionary. You would help me remember that Jesus is my best friend.

(*Conclude by singing "This Little Gospel Light of Mine." Invite the congregation to join you.*)

Hands

THE BAPTISM OF OUR LORD:
Is. 42:1–7; Acts 10:34–38; Mark 1:4–11

Text. I, the Lord, have called you in righteousness; I will take hold of your hand. I will keep you and will make you to be a covenant for the people and a light for the Gentiles, to open eyes that are blind, to free captives from prison, and to release from the dungeon those who sit in darkness. *Is. 42:6–7*

Teaching aid. A large hand, outlined on and cut from cardboard. Tape hand to a ruler. (*Note: Consider practicing this message, having someone play the role of the children, before making the presentation.*)

Gospel nugget. God reached out to His people and rescued them with the life, death, and resurrection of Jesus Christ.

I'll make a deal with you. If you stay with me for this message, I promise that we'll have a good time. Is it a deal? Let's shake on it. (*Shake hands with several children.*)
In a way, God made a deal and shook hands with His people. When He chose the children of Israel to be His people, He told them that He would take care of them. He would be their God, and they would be His people. Then He sent them different signs to show them what a wonderful deal He gave them. They got God's love free, and they could use it anytime they wanted. Through Jesus He made the same deal with us, too. God has made us His children. He cares for us and expects us to care for others. That's where our hands come in, helping hands. By helping others we can thank God for loving us. In what ways can you use your hands to help someone? (*Encourage responses.*)
Now I want to talk about this hand (*show cardboard hand*). Every time I hold up this cardboard hand, I want all of you to

say, "hands." Let's try it a few times. (*Hold up hand several times for children to respond.*)

One of the first times the Bible speaks about (*raise cardboard hand and wait for response*) is in Lev. 9:22, where it says, "Then Aaron lifted his (*raise hand*) toward the people and blessed them." Aaron was God's servant, and he lifted his (*raise hand*) to bless God's people.

Jesus used His (*raise hand*), too. Listen to Luke 4:40: "When the sun was setting, the people brought to Jesus all who had various kinds of sickness, and laying His (*raise hand*) on each one, He healed them." In addition to using His (*raise hand*) to heal sick people, Jesus placed His loving (*raise hand*) on children just like you. Listen to Matt. 19:13: "Then little children were brought to Jesus for Him to place His (*raise hand*) on them and pray for them." Jesus used His (*raise hand*) to bless and pray for children. How kind He was!

There was a time when the disciple Peter really needed a hand from Jesus. We hear about it in Matt. 14:29–31: " 'Come,' [Jesus] said. Then Peter got down out of the boat, walked on the water and came toward Jesus. But when [Peter] saw the wind, he was afraid and, beginning to sink, cried out, 'Lord, save me!' Immediately Jesus reached out His hand and caught him." Jesus saved Peter from drowning.

Jesus' (*raise hand*) were also hurt. Where did the Roman soldiers put the spikes when they nailed Jesus to the cross? (*Raise hand*). Yes. Later, when Jesus' disciple Thomas couldn't believe that Jesus was alive again, Jesus invited Thomas to touch the holes in His (*raise hand*), where the spikes had been.

Jesus often used His (*raise hand*) to serve people. His touch worked many miracles, and He never used His (*raise hand*) for anything but love.

Now let's give God a hand, too.

Prayer. Thank You, Lord, for making us Your people (*lead children in clapping*). We promise to serve you with our (*raise hand*). Amen.

Never Too Young

EPIPHANY 2: *1 Sam. 3:1–10; 1 Cor. 6:12–20; John 1:43–51*

Text. So Eli told Samuel, "Go and lie down, and if He calls you, say, 'Speak, LORD, for your servant is listening.'" So Samuel went and lay down in his place. *1 Sam. 3:9*

Teaching aid. Driver's license.

Gospel nugget. God provides servants of all ages to proclaim His Word.

(*Show driver's license to children.*) This is my driver's license. Terrible picture of me, isn't it? May I see your driver's license? You don't have one? Why not? You don't know how to drive yet, and you're still too young to learn.

Do grown-ups sometimes say you're too young to do things? What are you too young to do? (*Invite answers.*) Yes, I guess you'll have to wait awhile before you do things like get a job or get married. But there are many things you can do well right now.

Did you know that God uses children to serve His people? Today you heard a Bible reading about Samuel. Many people had forgotten about the Lord at the time Samuel lived. But Samuel's mother knew the Lord, and she wanted her son to know Him, too. She sent Samuel to learn about God from a man named Eli. One night, while sleeping, Samuel heard someone calling his name. Samuel thought it was Eli, but it wasn't. Again he heard someone calling him. Once more Samuel went to Eli and asked, "What do you want?" Eli said, "I didn't call you, Samuel. Go back to bed." Samuel went back to bed. But the same thing happened a third time. Finally, Eli realized that God was calling Samuel's name and that God had a special job for young Samuel. The Lord God would train Samuel as a special minister.

Another boy, whose name we don't know, became famous for trusting Jesus. One day, more than 5,000 people gathered to hear Jesus teach. Jesus wanted to give them lunch, but there wasn't enough money to buy food for 5,000 people. A boy in the crowd had brought a lunch of 5 pieces of bread and 2 fish. His mother probably expected him to finish it all by himself, but he shared it with Jesus. Jesus performed a miracle with those 5 pieces of bread and 2 fish. He fed all 5,000 people with that little bit of food.

As you can see from these true stories, God doesn't think that children are too young to help Him. Helping God do His work is the most important thing people can do, no matter how old they are.

I don't think you can expect God to awaken you in the middle of the night with some special message, but we can all share our food with hungry people. Jesus lives in you. He worked for us by suffering for our sins. He carried off our sins to make us perfect in God's sight. Now He wants you to work for Him. We want to work for Jesus because He is our Savior.

What things might you do for Jesus? (*Invite responses.*) Young people most often work for Jesus by helping others. Since they know how much Jesus loves them, they want to love others, too. Praying is another job for you. God wants us to pray for all people—the sick or sad, those who don't know about Him, for friends and relatives, even those people who don't like us!

You have important work ahead of you. And no matter your age, you're old enough because Jesus lives in you, and He will help you.

Prayer. Dear Lord, we are workers for You. Help us to know what to do and how to do it. Help us lead others to Your love. In Jesus' name we pray. Amen.

Second Chance for Jonah

EPIPHANY 3: Jonah 3:1–5, 10; 1 Cor. 7:29–31; Mark 1:14–20

Text. When God saw what they did and how they turned from their evil ways, He had compassion and did not bring upon them the destruction He had threatened. *Jonah 3:10*

Teaching aid. Draw a simple map on a large sheet of paper. Place a line between two points marked HERE and THERE. Place an *X* near the point marked HERE.

Gospel nugget. God patiently extends His love even to those who persistently resist Him.

Today we're going to read a map. I drew this map with two cities on it. One city is named HERE, and the other is called THERE. I also drew a road connecting the two cities. This *X* stands for the place we are right now. As you can see, we are closer to HERE than to THERE. Suppose I told you to travel from the *X* to the city called HERE. It's an exciting and huge city filled with people who can do just about anything they please. However, the citizens of HERE don't like strangers, and you are strangers. In fact, they beat up and killed the last visitors. Would you rather go HERE or THERE? (*Invite a response from an older child.*) Yes, I would be tempted to go to THERE instead, even though it's farther away.

That's exactly what Jonah did. You might remember that once Jonah was swallowed by a large fish. He lived inside it for three days before the fish spit him up on the seashore. But do you know why that fish swallowed Jonah? He disobeyed God.

Jonah's job was to tell people in a city called Nineveh that God was angry with them. They must change their ways! But Jonah was afraid of Nineveh's people, so he decided to get on a boat going the other direction. A terrible storm arose, and Jonah realized that he couldn't escape from God. He was tossed over the side of the ship. That's when the fish swallowed him. God gave Jonah some time to think about obeying His directions. Finally, Jonah went to Nineveh.

Sometimes we feel like running away from God. Anytime we do something the wrong way, it's like trying to escape from Him. Let me tell you a story to show what I mean.

Mom told Matthew to pick up his toys. But Matthew wasn't quite ready to do what Mom asked. He decided to play with the dog first. Then he spent some time snacking on pretzels, whistling to the birds outside his window, checking to see if the TV worked, examining the hole in his sock, scratching an itch on his ankle, tying knots in his shoe laces, counting the books on his shelf, and making faces at the cat. He did everything except pick up his toys. Mom was angry with Matthew, with good reason. She would not allow him to play with his toys for two whole days. You see, God places moms and dads in charge of children, and He expects children to obey their parents. So when Matthew decided not to do what his mother asked, he was like Jonah—going the wrong way.

Now I have a serious question for you. Did Matthew's mother show that she didn't love Matthew when she punished him? Not at all. Matthew suffered because he did wrong, not because his mom didn't love him. How about Jonah? Did Jonah get swallowed by that fish because God hated him? Not at all. Instead, when Jonah was going the wrong way, God used a giant fish to stop him, turn him around, and spit him in the right direction. God loved Jonah. He loves you and me, too. He forgives us when we do wrong, and He helps us do what is right.

Prayer. Thank You, Lord, for being so patient. Give us the power to follow You and to do what You want. In Jesus' name we pray. Amen.

Words in Your Mouth

EPIPHANY 4: Deut. 18:15–20; 1 Cor. 8:1–13; Mark 1:21–28

Text. I will raise up for them a prophet like you from among their brothers; I will put My words in his mouth, and he will tell them everything I command him. *Deut. 18:18*

Teaching aid. One reliable, confident child. Also, a Bible.

Gospel nugget. God still makes available in Jesus Christ His true Word.

I'm going to ask (*child's name*) to help me today. When I whisper a message in your ear, (*child's name*), I want you to say it out loud to the other children. (*Whisper the following:*) "Jesus loves you." (*Pause for child to repeat message.*)
(*Whisper:*) "Jesus knows you by name." (*Pause for child to repeat message.*)
(*Whisper:*) "He made you His child." (*Pause for child to repeat message.*)
Thank you, (*child's name*), for telling everyone that important message.
Long ago God told Moses about the many people who would speak for God to the children of Israel. Those people were called prophets. (*Read text.*) Some of the prophets were Samuel, Elijah, Huldah, Isaiah, and Ezekiel. Many years passed before the best prophet of all, Jesus Himself, spoke to the people.
Those who speak for God we now call ministers. There are many different kinds of ministers, but they all are alike in one way. True ministers tell others what God says. They know what

God says by reading the Bible (*indicate Bible*). We learn the Bible at church and Sunday school. Let's see how you could be a minister if someone asked you the following questions:

What would you say if someone asked you how the world began? (*Allow time for children's response.*) That's correct. God created the world and everything in it.

What if someone asked you who Noah was? (*Invite responses.*) Yes, God told Noah to build a huge boat, an ark, to save his family and each kind of animal.

What if someone asked, "Why do you celebrate Christmas?" (*Encourage responses.*) That one is easy, isn't it? Jesus our Savior was born.

What if your friend asked how to be forgiven of her sins? (*Allow response.*) Yes. Jesus forgives people who admit their sins and ask Him for forgiveness. You seem to know what ministers need to know.

Now let's talk about how God's ministers act. This question is for those who go to school. What would you do if the person sitting next to you at lunch forgot his sandwich and was hungry? (*Encourage responses.*) That person would really appreciate your sharing some of your lunch. If he asked why you're so kind, you could say that God blessed you with enough food to share with others.

God made you the way you are. All the good answers you gave to those questions a few moments ago came from God. He gave you faith in Jesus and placed Jesus in your hearts. With Jesus in your heart, you know right from wrong and good from bad. You know how to show your love for Jesus by treating people the same way Jesus does. You know where to go for forgiveness.

To end our time together this morning, let's say some special words that Jesus taught His apostles to say to their friends. I'll whisper the words, and you repeat them out loud: "Now may the Lord of peace Himself (*pause*) give you peace at all times (*pause*) and in every way (*pause*). The Lord be with all of you." (*Pause.*) Amen. [*2 Thess. 3:16*]

Look on the Bright Side

EPIPHANY 5: *Job 7:1-7; 1 Cor. 9:16-23; Mark 1:29-39*

Text. Does not man have hard service on earth? Are not his days like those of a hired man? *Job 7:1*

Teaching aid. A toaster.

Gospel nugget. Sadness, hardship, and trouble lose their capacity to destroy when viewed in the light of the Gospel.

How many of you ever had a very bad day? (*Note response.*) Me too. Mine was last Friday, and it all began with this toaster. It just wouldn't cooperate. First, it ate the bread. Well, at least it wouldn't give back the bread I put in it. The burning toast smelled up the kitchen something awful. After I took the toaster apart and adjusted a little spring, it gave the bread back. Too bad I wasn't in the next room to catch it. Shot that bread right through the kitchen door and onto my dog who was sleeping by the couch. The hot bread caused my dog to yip, and he took off running—right into my huge potted cactus, which fell over. I decided not to pick up the cactus until I ate my toast. Then I remembered that the toaster didn't work. What a way to start a day!

My little story isn't exactly true, but it's a good story to tell when talking about bad days (or bad months or bad years).

The Bible story about Job is also about bad days. It's not funny, but it does have a happy ending.

Job was very rich and happy. He had 10 children, and he

owned 7,000 sheep, 3,000 camels, and at least a thousand other kinds of animals. Many servants did whatever Job commanded.

Then one day, things started going wrong. First, Job's enemies attacked and killed his servants who were working in the farm fields. Next, fire fell from the sky and burned up all of Job's sheep and shepherds. Then robbers stole all of Job's camels and killed more servants. As if that weren't enough, a strong wind blew down the house where Job's children were having a party. All his children died. I imagine Job was very sad. How he must have cried!

Job had more troubles. He often felt disappointed, lonely, and forgotten by God. Even his friends couldn't help him. No matter how bad life got for Job, he had one hope, one thing he could trust—God's promises. What do you think Job said about all his sadness and pain? He said, "The Lord gave and the Lord has taken away; may the name of the Lord be praised" (Job 1:21). Job trusted that God would take care of him, even if he died.

God stayed with Job. After much suffering and sickness, Job got better. He became twice as rich as before. He had 10 more children and lived to be 140.

When we think of sad stories with happy endings, we must also think about Jesus. During the week before He died, Jesus was arrested and beaten. People made fun of Him. Even His best friends ran away from Him. Jesus was sentenced to die like a criminal. He was tortured and killed on the cross. He suffered all that to take away our sins.

But there was a bright side. Maybe you know about it. Jesus rose from the dead and lives today in heaven, where He is waiting for us.

Next time you have a very bad day, think about Job and Jesus and their very bad days. Jesus, our Savior, can give bad days happy endings. No matter what happens, even if we die, Jesus will give us more happiness than we ever knew before.

Prayer. Dear Lord, help us to see the bright side when things go bad. Help us trust You, whatever happens. In Jesus' name we pray. Amen.

Too Simple?

EPIPHANY 6: 2 Kings 5:1–14; 1 Cor. 9:24–27; Mark 1:40–45

Text. Naaman's servants went to him and said, "My father, if the prophet had told you to do some great thing, would you not have done it? How much more, then, when he tells you, 'Wash and be cleansed!' " *2 Kings 5:13*

Teaching aid. A Sunday bulletin placed near the location where children gather for the message.

Gospel nugget. God grants His grace without any merit or worth on the part of believers.

Look here. Somebody left a church bulletin. I should get it to the ushers in the back of church. Let's see now, how should I get it back there? I know! I'll put it in my pocket and mail it after church. Isn't that a good idea? Oh, I guess there is another way. Hmm. I can pass it back. I'll give it to the first person in this row and ask him (her) to pass it down until it gets to the end of the row. That person can give it to the person behind him who then can pass it down that row until it gets to the end. Then that person hands it to the person behind him who can pass it down that row . . . There must be a simpler way to get this bulletin to the ushers. Does anyone have a suggestion? (*Consider suggestions.*) Okay. We need only one person to carry it back to the ushers. Will you do it? Thanks. (*Wait for child to return.*)

Did you hear the name of Naaman in the today's Bible reading? Naaman had a problem, too. His problem also had a simple solution, but he didn't know it. Listen to Naaman's problem.

Naaman was sick with leprosy, a skin disease. A little slave girl in Naaman's house told Naaman's wife about a prophet in Israel who could heal people with leprosy. Naturally, Naaman rushed off to this prophet, whose name was Elisha. Naaman asked Elisha to cure his leprosy. Elisha said, "Go, wash yourself seven times in the Jordan [River], and your flesh will be restored and you will be cleansed" (*2 Kings 5:10*). Naaman was surprised by Elisha's cure because it sounded so simple. Too simple. Naaman probably expected to swallow some yucky tasting medicine or to do some painful exercises, or pay a lot of money to be cured. But Elisha told him just to dip himself in the nearby river seven times, and he would be healed. No charge.

Now Naaman was angry! He traveled many miles and over many rivers much closer to home just to take a bath in the Jordan River! Finally, Naaman did what Elisha suggested. His leprosy went away, and he went home a healthy man. The simple cure for leprosy worked because God made it work.

Sometimes we Christians are like Naaman. We want Jesus to save us from our sins so we can go to heaven. Jesus tells us that forgiveness and heaven are free gifts. Really free gifts. But all that sounds too simple.

Maybe we're not used to really free gifts. Some gas stations give away free drinking glasses. You don't have to pay for the glasses, but you do have to buy lots of gasoline before they give you a glass.

God's gifts are different. They are truly free. Forgiveness is a gift. So is heaven. We can't do a thing to earn them. It's a good thing that Jesus is so free with these gifts, too. Is there ever a day when we don't need forgiveness? We never have a perfect day. There is no limit to how many times He'll forgive us.

Prayer. Thank You, dear God, for sending Jesus, who suffered, died, was buried, and rose from the grave to give us Your free gifts. Help us to believe for Jesus' sake. Amen.

He Doesn't Remember

EPIPHANY 7: Is. 43:18–25; 2 Cor. 1:18–22; Mark 2:1–12

Text. I, even I, am He who blots out your transgressions, for My own sake, and remembers your sins no more. *Is. 43:25*

Teaching aid. In advance, in large letters write "God remembers your sins no more" on a strip of paper. Bring along a black marker.

Gospel nugget. God forgives and forgets our sins for Jesus' sake.

Who can read this slip of paper? (*Allow an older child to read.*) Let's say those words together a few times. (*Display message while repeating it.*)

Now I'm going to take this black marker and blot out the word *sins*. See? The word *sins* is gone. When God forgives our sins, it's as if He takes a big marker and blots them out and then forgets them.

Have you ever heard anyone say "forgive and forget"? What does that mean? Yes, it means that you aren't angry and won't even remember the wrong that someone does against you. Forgiving AND forgetting can be hard to do. Let me give you an example.

Pretend that while you and your friend, Lisa, are playing catch, she throws the ball over your head on purpose. You have to chase the ball a long way. Then Lisa throws the ball over your head a second time, and you have to chase it again. Now you feel angry and hurt because Lisa is treating you this way, and you begin to cry. Lisa comes to you, puts her hand on your shoulder, and says, "I'm sorry. We're such good friends that I really want you to forgive me."

You answer, "I forgive you, Lisa, but I won't forget what happened. If you ever throw the ball over my head again, I won't be your friend!" Sometimes it's easy to forgive, but very hard to forget when someone is mean or hurts us.

Now let's think about how God's forgiveness works. Suppose you do something wrong over and over again. Maybe it's something like calling your friend names. We know that God wants us to treat others with love and respect, so calling our friend names is against God's will. Every time you say those nasty names, you end up asking both your friend and God to forgive you. You hope they forgive you and forget what you have done because you really love both God and your friend. After awhile, though, your friend may tire of forgiving you. You might even lose that person as your friend. But God never tires of forgiving us when we come to Him over and over and over and over again. Each time we ask God to forgive us, He does—over and over again, and He forgets our sin too.

It's not that God has a bad memory. He remembers the important things. He always remembers your name and that you need Him. You're one of the reasons He sent Jesus to earth on the first Christmas. He remembers that Jesus lived the kind of life God wants for all of His people. God remembers what happened at 3 o'clock one dark Friday afternoon when His Son died for your sins. And God remembers how early on Easter morning He took His Son out of the grave and gave Him new life, because He loves all of us. That's what He remembers. But when He forgives us, He never remembers our sins.

Let's praise God for remembering to love us. Let's sing together "Jesus Loves Me." (*Sing first verse.*)

Now let's pray.

Prayer. Dear God, forgive us for all the times that we have done wrong. Thank You for not remembering our sin. Please help us to be more like Jesus. Make it easier for us to forgive and forget. In His name we pray. Amen.

Best Friends

EPIPHANY 8: Hos. 2:14–16 (17–18), 19–20; 2 Cor. 3:1b–6; Mark 2:18–22

Text. I will betroth you to me forever; I will betroth you in righteousness and justice, in love and compassion. I will betroth you in faithfulness, and you will acknowledge the LORD. *Hos. 2:19–20*

Teaching aid. Wedding, engagement, or friendship ring (or other token of esteem).

Gospel nugget. God forgives sinners and in love tells them when they are wrong.

Who has a good friend? (*Invite children to name their good friends.*) Are any of you married (engaged, dating, etc.) to your good friend? My friend and I wear one of these (*display ring*) to show that we're even more than friends. We love each other enough to be married (engaged, good friends, etc.).

Our best friend is Jesus. That's why the Bible talks about Christians as being married to Jesus. The Bible calls Jesus the Bridegroom, and it calls the Christian church—you and me—His bride.

Jesus loves us more than anyone else loves us. It's good to be best friends with someone who loves us so much. How long do you think Jesus' love will last? The Bible says, "Give thanks to the LORD Almighty, for the LORD is good; His love endures [lasts] forever" (Jer. 33:11).

Forever is a long time. Some people in our church have been married 5, 15, 25, even 50 years. Others have been friends for more years than they can remember. But even that is not forever. Jesus loves us forever; He never stops being our best friend.

The reason that we're such close friends with our Savior is

because He always forgives us. No matter what we do wrong, we can count on Jesus to say, "I forgive you."

What are some ways in which you have done wrong? (*Invite responses.*) Oh, there are so many ways to sin! Sometimes you might be mean to friends or brothers or sisters. Perhaps you haven't done a few things that Mom or Dad asked you to do. Maybe you were noisy while they were talking on the telephone. Or perhaps you didn't pick up your toys. At times like those, you need to talk to Jesus.

How do you talk with Jesus? (*Wait for a child to respond.*) We talk to Him when we pray. And Jesus listens, too! He is such a special friend that He always answers us when we pray. How do you think Jesus answers when we ask Him to take us to heaven when we die? I think He says, "That's why I'm your best friend. I want us all to live together in heaven. I'm getting a place ready for you now."

Jesus does another thing for those He loves. He tells them when they're wrong. We may not always like to know when we're wrong, but we need to know when we sin. If we didn't, we might forget Him or stop believing in Him. Thank God that Jesus doesn't let us get away. Just when we have misbehaved, Jesus reminds us that we belong to Him. How good it is to hear Him say, "Hey! I'm your best friend, remember? I'm always ready to forgive you. Let's be friends forever!"

Now is a good time to thank our best Friend. Will you pray with me?

Prayer. Dear Jesus, thank You for always loving me. Even when I'm not a very good friend to You, You are my best Friend. If ever I forget You, please call me back. Don't let me live a single day without Your love. Amen.

Let Me Do It!

TRANSFIGURATION: 2 Kings 2:1–12c; 2 Cor. 3:12–4:2; Mark 9:2–9

Text. When they had crossed, Elijah said to Elisha, "Tell me, what can I do for you before I am taken from you?"

"Let me inherit a double portion of your spirit," Elisha replied (*2 Kings 2:9*).

Teaching aid. Dust cloth, small battery-operated vacuum cleaner, empty offering baskets, and a piece of sheet music.

Gospel nugget. The Lord provides and empowers enthusiastic ministers for His people.

What kind of jobs do you do for Mom or Dad? (*Invite responses.*) What kind of jobs do you do at school for your teacher? (*Encourage responses.*) What do the kids say when the teacher asks, "Who will do a special job for me?" Many kids eagerly volunteer. Well, since you seem to have on-the-job experience, who wants to help me with a few special cleaning jobs? (*Enlist volunteers and direct them to tasks.*) That bench (pew) over there looks a little dusty so wipe it with this dust cloth. This vacuum cleaner will help with cleaning the carpet. Who knows how to work it? I have some empty offering baskets that should be stored in the back of the church. Will you take them? And finally, our organist (pianist) needs this music. Could you run it over to her (him)?

(*As volunteers are completing the tasks, speak with the other children and the congregation.*) I'm glad we have so many willing workers this morning. Why, we have more workers than we can use. I think they're just about finished with their tasks. Let's get together again for our message.

I would like you to know about two famous workers from

the Bible, Elijah and Elisha. Elijah's job for many years was to tell people what God said. Elijah was very good at his job, but he was getting old. God wanted Elijah to come to heaven, and He wanted Elijah's friend, Elisha, to take over Elijah's work. Of course, Elisha didn't want to see his old friend leave. So Elisha followed Elijah everywhere. Elisha wanted to do everything his friend had done, and more. When the time came for Elijah to leave, he wanted to give Elisha a special gift. So he asked Elisha, "What can I give you?"

Elisha answered, "I want to do twice as much for God and His people. So, please give me twice as much of your strength." Elisha was eager to do God's work.

A similar thing happened many years later. One day, Jesus climbed a mountain with three disciples, Peter, James, and John. An astonishing thing happened. Suddenly, Jesus' clothes turned whiter than snow, and a booming voice spoke out. It was God Himself! God said, "This is my Son, whom I love. Listen to Him."

Jesus and the three disciples came down from the mountain, eager to begin working for God's people. The disciples wanted to be like their friend, Jesus. It was almost as if they were saying, "Let me work for You. Let me do it!" Jesus knew that His job was to suffer and die for sinners. He was the only one who could do that job. But before He went to heaven, Jesus taught the disciples what they could do for God, and soon after He gave them His Holy Spirit. Peter, James, John, and the other disciples told others about Jesus. They healed people and forgave sins in Jesus' name. They traveled to many towns, telling people about the Savior.

Jesus has also given you His Holy Spirit so you can do His work, too. Tell others about Him. How good it is to work for someone who loves us so much!

Prayer. Thank You, Lord God, for giving us hands, feet, mouths, brains, and hearts. Thank You also for giving us Your Holy Spirit. Help us use all that we have to serve You. Make us as eager and strong to do Your work as Elisha, Peter, James, and John. Amen.

So Sorry

ASH WEDNESDAY: Joel 2:12–19; 2 Cor. 5:20b–6:2; Matt. 6:1–6, 16–21

Text. Rend your heart and not your garments. Return to the Lord, your God, for He is gracious and compassionate, slow to anger and abounding in love, and He relents from sending calamity. *Joel 2:13*

Teaching aid. A piece of cloth easy to tear.

Gospel nugget. The Lord Jesus invites repentance and graciously forgives all sins.

What do you do when you're upset about something? Do you yell and scream and stomp your feet? Maybe you get really quiet and go off by yourself. Perhaps you make faces or clench your fists or grind your teeth.

People living in Bible times did an odd thing when they became upset about their sins. Watch. (*Tear the cloth.*) They ripped their clothing. Sometimes they dressed in rags and smeared themselves with ashes to show how bad they felt about sinning. They were sorry that they had disobeyed God, but they were also glad they could tell God when they sinned instead of trying to hide their sins from Him.

Often, we don't want others to know when we do wrong. We might even be tempted to lie and say, "I didn't do anything." Sometimes people try to hide their sins from God. But God knows when each person does wrong.

And God gives His people a special gift to help us know when we have done wrong. He gives us consciences so we will know when we need forgiveness. Your conscience makes you feel your guilt. Sometimes it makes you afraid. God's people also need to ask, "What would Jesus want us to do? What would He say?"

When you know you've done wrong, don't run from God; instead run to Him. Repent. Repent means being sorry for your sins and asking God to forgive you because Jesus died for your sins. When you repent, you never want to sin again. You ask Jesus to help you fight sin.

As I mentioned before, people living in Bible times ripped their garments, or clothing, when they were sorry for sinning. Now listen to the prophet Joel, who told his people to do something else. (*Read text.*) Joel told the people to feel sorry for sinning. In a way he said, "Rip sin from your hearts so that you don't want to sin any more. Repent!"

What does God do if we tell Him our sins? Does He get mad at us or hate us? Joel answered that the Lord is "slow to anger and abounding in love." God forgives us. Not just once. Not just twice. But every time we repent. We can really be glad to be able to tell God when we sin.

Something else needs to happen when we repent. John the Baptist once said, "Produce fruit in keeping with repentance" (*Matt. 3:8*). John means that we should do good for others just as Jesus does good for us. Perhaps the most important good we can do is to forgive others when they wrong us.

Does it ever seem like you need to repent every day? Good! That's what God wants us to do. He knows that we just can't completely avoid sin. He knows our weaknesses. God doesn't expect us to rip our clothes and rub ashes on ourselves. Instead, He wants us to repent. After all, He sent Jesus to save sinners. Because He sent Jesus for you and me, when we say we're sorry, we know for sure that He forgives us.

Prayer. Dear God, thank You for giving us consciences. Help us know when to repent. Give us Your Holy Spirit to help us fight sin. Thank You for always hearing us when we say, "Please forgive me." We pray in Jesus' name. Amen.

Give Up

LENT 1: Gen. 22:1–18; Rom. 8:31–39; Mark 1:12–15

Text. Through your offspring all nations on earth will be blessed. *Gen. 22:18a*

Teaching aid. An object representing something that you would find difficult to give up (coffee, favorite soft drink or food, book, recorded music, hobby, art object, special gift, etc.)

Gospel nugget. God sacrificed His only Son to save sinners.

One of my favorite things is _____ . (*Show object and tell why it's your favorite thing.*) What are your favorite things? (*Encourage each child to respond.*) I think it would be hard to give up anything we like so much. We'll talk more about giving up favorite things in a few moments.

Today is the first Sunday of Lent. Lent is a season of the church year just like spring is a season of our calendar year. During Lent, we think about how Jesus gave up His life for sinners. Some Christians observe Lent by giving up their favorite things. I would give up _____ . The Bible doesn't say that Christians must give up something for Lent. But today's Bible story tells how God commanded Abraham to give up his only son, Isaac. It began as a frightening story.

Abraham and his wife, Sarah, wanted a child for many years. They didn't have their first child until they were very old. They named their baby son Isaac, and they loved him very much. When Isaac was a little older, God commanded Abraham to do something very difficult. God told Abraham to give up Isaac to God. Abraham's faith and trust in God were so strong that he was willing to do what God wanted. The story ended happily, though.

God allowed Abraham to keep Isaac, and He gave Abraham's family many blessings.

You already know the other famous story about giving up. It's the story we think about most at this time of year. What did God give up during the first Lent? John 3:16 says, "For God so loved the world that He gave His one and only Son, that whoever believes in Him shall not perish but have eternal life." That Bible passage has so many important words! God loved the world. He gave His only Son. Believers will live forever.

God gave up His one and only Son. What did Jesus give up? He gave up His life. Jesus could have been the most powerful king in the world, but He knew what His job was on earth. He gave up His life to take away our sins.

What does the Bible tell us to give up? God's word tells us to give up sin. God wants us to think about all the good we can do instead of all the bad things we're tempted to do. When other children are calling some other child ugly names, what does God expect from us? God expects us to defend the other person and to show kindness. What happens when we're tempted to steal something from a store when no one is looking? God expects us to give up our desire to steal and to be honest.

Oh yes, God wants us to give up one final thing. He wants us to just plain "give up." If you were wrestling, and your friend held your arms and legs and whole body so that you couldn't even move, you would probably shout something like, "I give up! I give up!" God wants us to say "I give up" every time we know that we are sinners, all tied up in evil. He wants us to give up and ask for His help, because we can't beat sin all by ourselves. Jesus did that for us. He rescued us from the devil and makes us holy in God's sight. Someday we'll live with all other Christians who give up and trust Jesus.

Prayer. Dear Heavenly Father, thank You for giving up Your holy Son, Jesus, as a sacrifice for our sins. Dear Jesus, thank You for giving up Your life on the cross to pay for our sins. Help us to give up all things that make You unhappy. We pray in Your name. Amen.

Promises Kept

LENT 2: Gen. 28:10–17, (18–22); Rom. 5:1–11; Mark 8:31–38

Text. There above it [ladder ascending to heaven] stood the LORD, and He said: "I am the LORD, the God of your father Abraham and the God of Isaac. I will give you and your descendants the land on which you are lying. Your descendants will be like the dust of the earth, and you will spread out to the west and to the east, to the north and to the south. All peoples on earth will be blessed through you and your offspring." *Gen. 28:13–14*

Teaching aid. A baby jar or small glass filled with dry soil or sand and a piece of heavy paper or cardboard in a contrasting color, against which the grains of soil will be easily visible. Also a pebble or small stone for each anticipated participant.

Gospel nugget. God's promises about what salvation brings in the future extend hope to His people.

We're going to make a little mess and a big guess today. First, the mess . . . (*Pour soil on paper.*) See how the soil in this glass is made up of little pieces. Those pieces are called dust, or grains. (*Pour soil back into glass.*) Now for the big guess: guess how many pieces of dust are in this glass. My guess is that there are so many grains that we couldn't count all of them. Think about how much dust there is in all the fields in the world!

God once promised Jacob that the people in his family would be as many as the "dust of the earth." That meant that Jacob's family would be very big and last a long, long time. But that wasn't the best news. God also promised that all people on earth would be blessed because of Jacob's family. He knew that Jesus would be part of Jacob's family. What a wonderful promise!

God made this promise to Jacob in a dream. In this dream angels were walking up and down a stairway. God talked to Jacob from the top of the stairway. Jacob was probably glad to hear God's promise, because he felt all alone that night when he went to sleep. He was far from home, traveling to a strange land to live with his uncle.

God's promises always come at the right times. The very first promise God ever made came right after Adam and Eve had sinned and had to leave the Garden of Eden. How do you think they felt about leaving their beautiful home? Yes, they were probably sad. Maybe they wondered whether God still loved them after they sinned. That's when God promised that He would send Jesus to take away sins.

Jesus made promises, also. Two criminals were put to death with Jesus on Good Friday. One criminal insulted Jesus. The other criminal asked Jesus to remember him. Jesus promised the criminal who wanted to be remembered that they would be together in heaven.

Did Jesus leave any promises for us? The Bible reports that Jesus promised always to be with His people. We're especially happy about this promise when we're sick or frightened. But Jesus is also with us when we're healthy and safe. He's with us when we're sleeping. Jesus is with us right now, giving us faith to believe His promises.

When Jacob woke up, he stacked up some stones, to help him remember God's promise. He named the place Bethel, which means "House of God." I want each of you to have a small rock. Take it home and place it where you'll see it. This rock will help you remember that God also lives at your house. Remember, He will always be with you.

Prayer. Dear God, thank You for keeping Your promise to give us Jesus. We're happy that He's with us right now. Help us trust Your promise the same way the dying thief trusted Jesus. We look forward to being with You in heaven. Amen.

How to Be Happy

LENT 3: *Ex. 20:1–17; 1 Cor. 1:22–25; John 2:13–22*

Text. You shall have no other gods before Me . . . You shall not misuse the name of the LORD your God . . . Remember the Sabbath day by keeping it holy. Honor your father and your mother, so that you may live long in the land the LORD your God is giving you. You shall not murder. You shall not commit adultery. You shall not steal. You shall not give false testimony against your neighbor. You shall not covet your neighbor's house. You shall not covet your neighbor's wife, or his manservant or maidservant, his ox or donkey, or anything that belongs to your neighbor. *Ex. 20:3, 7, 8, 12–17*

Teaching aid. Several books with impressive titles and the Bible.

Gospel nugget. Jesus perfectly obeyed all of God's laws in our stead, and the Holy Spirit enables us to live godly lives in the name of Jesus.

I have been looking for a book that tells how to live a happy life. Let's see if any of these library books will tell me how to live happily. (*Read titles of all books except the Bible.*) None of them sounds too promising. Here is one last book (the Bible). Its title is "How to be Happy!" (*Show it to a child who reads.*) Am I right? (*Encourage child to correct you.*) Oh, it's the Bible. I read something in here that made me believe it's a book on happy living. Listen. (*Read text above.*)

These are the Ten Commandments. God gives them to us

because He wants people to know what pleases Him. God also wants us to be happy. How can rules make people happy? Let me tell you.

Have you noticed that some street corners have STOP signs? How can STOP signs make people happy? Cars won't run into each other if they obey STOP signs. People in cars are safe, and so are people crossing the streets. God's rules are something like STOP signs. They help us live together safely. Let's talk about a few.

One commandment says "Honor your father and your mother." Respect them. If we're respectful, we will also obey our parents. How can that make our parents happy? Yes, they won't get angry with us, and they'll thank God for such obedient children. How can respecting our parents make us happy? Doesn't it just feel good to obey God and to make others glad?

Let's think about another commandment, the eighth. "You shall not give false testimony against your neighbor." What that really means is that we shouldn't say bad things about people (even if those bad things are true). Just think how happy life would be if people talked about others the way they like to be talked about.

We Christians are most happy because, when Jesus comes back at the end of the world, He's not going to tell anybody the bad things we have done. It's not that any of us are so good that we always obey all the commandments. No matter how hard we try, we just can't be that good. Nevertheless, God is not going to tell the bad things we have done. Why not? Because Jesus obeyed every commandment perfectly for each of us, because we couldn't do it ourselves. God is going to talk about us as if we have kept the commandments perfectly, like Jesus. That's the greatest news in the world!

Prayer. Thank You, Heavenly Father, for letting us know how to live happy lives. We confess that we don't always live by Your holy rules. Thank You for sending Jesus to obey those rules for us, and for making us perfect and holy in Your sight. Amen.

Where to Look

LENT 4: Num. 21:4–9; Eph. 2:4–10; John 3:14–21

Text. So Moses made a bronze snake and put it up on a pole. Then when anyone was bitten by a snake and looked at the bronze snake, he lived. *Num. 21:9*

Teaching aid. A plain, wooden or metal cross hidden from view but easily accessible.

Gospel nugget. Sinners may always repent and look to the cross for salvation.

I would like to begin today's children's message, but I can't find the object I wanted to show you. I wish I knew whom to blame for losing it. Should I blame my wife (husband, child, friend). No, she's usually the one who finds what I lose. Perhaps the organist took it to hold down the pages of her (his) music. No, the organist would ask before borrowing anything. Do you think the cleaning people took it? Probably not. Oh, I should have stayed home today. I knew nothing would go right. Hey, do you think God might be playing mean tricks on me? No, I don't know of any time God ever played a mean trick on anyone. But I do know a scary story about Moses, God's people, and some snakes. Would you like to hear it?

God did so much for His people, the children of Israel. He helped them get away from some people who were *very* mean to them. God took care of them as they wandered through the desert for 40 years. Every day He even gave them food. But the children of Israel became tired of eating the same thing day after day. They complained to Moses. They even became angry with God, and they said some hateful things to Him. The children of Israel were very much in danger of refusing to believe in God. Then the snakes came. God sent snakes to remind the children of Israel that He was their God. He knew what was best for them right down to the very food they ate.

The snakes bit many people. Now the people forgot about little things like the food they disliked. They cried for help, because if a snake bit them, they would die. God heard their cries for help. He ordered Moses to build a statue of a snake and to place it high on a pole. After that, if those who had snakebite looked at the snake statue, they would live and not die.

I'm glad that snake story ended happily. We can also tell a story about you and me. The beginning isn't so good, but the ending is very happy. Oh, wow! Guess what? I just remembered where I left the object I wanted to show you. I'll get it. (*Get the cross, bring it back with you.*) See. It's a cross. I'll leave it right here where I won't misplace it again. Now back to the story about you and me. I'm a sinner, you know. You are, too. We sinners have some bad habits. We like to grumble and complain. God blesses us and gives us everything we really need, but we complain anyway. For example, God created the earth so that it would grow everything we need to eat. Yet we might get bored eating good food, or we might think God should have created nothing but ice cream.

We're blessed that God doesn't send snakes to remind us He's our loving God who knows what's best for us! But we don't need to be afraid of snakes. We really need to fear sin!

The Bible tells us that sin kills. Every time we sin it's like being bitten by a poisonous snake, but worse. Sin hurts us because it takes us away from God—and we can't live without Him. What are we to do?

(*Raise cross up high*) Look here. All sinners look up at the cross. You're saved! We look at Jesus, who died on the cross, and remember that Jesus saved us. Sin can't kill us. We are going to live forever with Jesus!

Old and New

LENT 5: Jer. 31:31–34; Heb. 5:7–9; John 12:20–33

Text. For I will forgive their wickedness and will remember their sins no more. *Jer. 31:34b*

Teaching aid. Several similar articles which contrast old and new or clean and unclean, such as two dishes—one stained with food and the other clean; two shirts—one clean and the other soiled; two pieces of paper—one crumpled and the other new.

Gospel nugget. God's New Testament covenant in Christ required faith alone to gain God's acceptance.

(*Involve children in a discussion of the following questions.*) Do you know the difference between old and new? (*Hold up dishes*) Which of these looks newer? Why do you think so? Yes, it's much cleaner, so it looks like it was never used. How about these two shirts, which looks newer? Yes, this other one is wrinkled and messy. Which piece of paper would you want if I asked you to draw a picture? Why wouldn't you want this crinkled piece? It's difficult to draw on this old piece. The new sheet is better. You made some good choices so far. Now think about choosing between games. One game has 4,358,962 rules and the other has only one. Which would you rather play? Me, too. A game with many rules may be too difficult to play and certainly hard to enjoy.

Long ago, before Jesus was born, God's people turned life into a game with too many rules, hoping to obey them and earn God's love. They thought that being good would save them from God's anger. How well do you think the people obeyed? They made many mistakes. Sometimes they even made mistakes on purpose because they didn't like some of rules.

God never stopped loving His people even though they

couldn't keep all the rules. Instead, He promised to send someone who could obey all the rules for the people. Who was that someone? Of course, it was Jesus. Jesus was like the difference between old and new.

God's old way for people to be saved from sin was never to sin in the first place. Impossible! Too many rules! God's new way of being saved is to receive a free gift. That gift is faith in Jesus, who obeyed all the rules that you and I can't keep. We don't do anything to make Jesus love us. He just does! And with His love comes forgiveness for all our sins and His promise to take us to heaven.

If we don't have to obey God's rules to get into heaven, why should we obey Him anyway? Think of it this way. Imagine two kids your age, Sally and Sam. Sam says to you, "If you want to be my friend, you have to give me two dollars every day." Sally says, "I'll be your friend just because I like you." Which of those two kids makes a better friend? Sally, for sure. And you would probably do everything you could to be a good friend to Sally, too. Sam's offer of friendship was selfish. He wanted something from you before he would be your friend. Jesus is an unselfish friend. He was so concerned about you that He took away your sins by suffering and dying on the cross. He still thinks about you all the time.

Let's thank God for loving us.

Prayer. We pray, Heavenly Father, that all people would know You as their best Friend. Thank You for sending Jesus to obey all the rules for us. We could never be perfect on our own. Help us love You back. Help us love others just as You love us. And when we fail to love You and other people, remind us to ask Your forgiveness. We know You will always be our Friend. Amen.

No Big Deal

PALM SUNDAY: Zech. 9:9–10; Phil. 2:5–11; Mark 14:1–15:47 or Mark 15:1–39

Text. Rejoice greatly, O Daughter of Zion! Shout, Daughter of Jerusalem! See, your king comes to you, righteous and having salvation, gentle and riding on a donkey, on a colt, the foal of a donkey. *Zech. 9:9*

Teaching aid. Address an envelope to yourself, and seal a five- or ten-dollar bill inside. Then deface the envelope (step on it with muddy feet, drive your car over it, crumple it, etc.)

Gospel nugget. Jesus humbly obeyed the Father to provide triumphant eternal life.

Do you ever get some mail? Perhaps you've had some envelopes addressed just to you at Christmas or on your birthday. Exciting, isn't it? I look forward to opening my mail. But the other day, I found this in my mail box (*reveal envelope*), and I still haven't opened it. By the way this envelope looks, it can't be anything important. But it is addressed to me, so I suppose I should see what's inside (*open envelope*). Wow, ten dollars! Someone sent me a ten-dollar gift in this banged-up old envelope. Would you have guessed this envelope contained a valuable gift? Me either. This surprise reminds me of Jesus on the first Palm Sunday.
Would you agree that Jesus was the most important person who ever lived? Yes, indeed. He was God's Son. His job was to save sinners by dying for them. Now, that's important, important enough to hold a parade in His honor. People lined the streets to see Jesus on that first Palm Sunday. They knew He did many miracles, and some people claimed he was God's Son. But who would expect God's Son to parade through town on a donkey?

Why, that seems to us like finding treasure in a beat-up envelope! We would like it better if someone as important as Jesus came to town on a proud white horse, surrounded by guards in fancy uniforms. But here was humble Jesus riding only a borrowed donkey. Today we celebrate Palm Sunday to remember how Jesus comes to the people and what He does for them.

Jesus did everything in plain and simple ways. Do you remember His birth? The angels welcomed Him by singing music fit for a king, but Jesus surely didn't look like a king. Mary dressed Him in strips of cloth. He slept in a box filled with hay.

Jesus spent His entire life doing good for others. Can you imagine how rich Jesus might have been if He had collected money for doing miracles? But Jesus never cared for money. He didn't even own a home. He wasn't a show-off either. Jesus didn't want to be famous because He could turn water into wine, cure sick people, or even raise people from the dead. He wanted people to know Him as their Savior, the only one who could take their sins away.

Do you remember how Jesus came into your life? He didn't wait for you to invite Him, and He didn't demand gifts or money from you or your parents. He simply said, "I know you. You are Mine." Then He performed a miracle. Jesus gave you faith so that you could believe in Him as your own Savior. And when all that happened, there was a joyful celebration. The angels celebrate every time someone new is added to God's family. Isn't that amazing? Now that you are part of God's family, you can praise the Lord, too. Let's celebrate as the people did on the first Palm Sunday. They shouted, "Hosanna!" Let's try it together: "Hosanna!" Louder now and happier, too: "Hosanna!" We'll say "Hosanna" three more time at the end of our prayer. Be ready.

Prayer. We praise You Lord Jesus, Son of God, Holy King. Although You came to be King, You were a humble servant to all sinners. Help us serve others as humble Christians, sharing Your love with all people. We pray in Your name. (*In a whisper to children*) "Ready?" (*Big sound*) HOSANNA! HOSANNA! HOSANNA!

Tears of Joy

EASTER: Is. 25:6–9; 1 Cor. 15:19–28; Mark 16:1–8 or John 20:1–9 (10–18)

Text. He will swallow up death forever. The Sovereign LORD will wipe away the tears from all faces; He will remove the disgrace of His people from all the earth. The LORD has spoken. In that day they will say, "Surely this is our God; we trusted in Him, and He saved us. This is the LORD we trusted in Him; let us rejoice and be glad in His salvation." *Is. 25:8, 9*

Teaching aid. Box of facial tissue.

Gospel nugget. Christians will live forever because Jesus defeated sin and death on Easter.

Happy Easter. Do you know what to say if I say, "He is risen?" All together now say, "He is risen indeed!" (*Practice the statement and response several times.*) Listen carefully because I'll say "He is risen" several times in the next few minutes. Each time I say, "He is risen," you answer, "He is risen indeed!" Have you ever felt really sad? Have you ever felt really happy? Have you ever quickly changed from feeling very sad to feeling very happy? We had a sad day in church last Friday. Though it was "Good Friday," we were unhappy because we remembered how Jesus suffered an awful death on the cross. He died for us. He suffered because you and I and everyone else are sinners. The only way for Him to take away our sins was to die.

But today is different! He is risen! (*Prompt children to respond.*) Very early on the Sunday after Jesus died, three of His friends celebrated the first Easter. They went to Jesus' tomb in the cemetery. (A tomb is like a small cave dug into some rock.) As you know, they discovered that Jesus' tomb was empty. Well, almost empty. An angel was inside. The angel said, "Jesus isn't here. He is risen!" (*Response*)

The three friends ran off to tell Jesus' disciples the good news. Jesus wasn't dead anymore. They had been crying because their friend died. Now they cried because they were so happy. Can you imagine the excitement when they said to the disciples, "He is risen?" (*Response*) Why, they probably jumped around shouting, "He is risen!" (*Response*) He is risen! (*Response*) He is risen! (*Response*) Christians all over the world are happy today because He is risen. (*Response*)

Easter makes us happy for ourselves, too. If you've ever been to a cemetery, you know it's not a very happy place. People do a lot of crying there because they miss someone who died. But cemeteries will empty out when Jesus returns at the end of the world. They'll be as empty as Jesus' tomb. Listen to what Isaiah says. (*Read text*). Because He is risen (*response*), all Christians will also come alive again and live with Jesus forever after they die. Christians will say, "I'm risen, too!" Can you imagine the happy celebration in heaven?

Easter is such a joyful Sunday, don't you wish we could celebrate it more often? Then every Sunday we could say, "He is risen!" (*Response*) Would you like to hear more good news? Every Sunday is like Easter. We can celebrate Easter in July, November, and January. Every Sunday is like Easter because we hear that Jesus will live forever and so will we!

Here is a tissue to carry with you today. Last Friday, when you remembered how Jesus died for us, you might have used this tissue to soak up sad tears rolling down your cheeks. Now we can cry tears of joy. Keep your tissues handy to remind yourself that He is risen. (*Response*)

Are you happy? Great. Let's see if the congregation is happy, too. You and I will tell them the good news, and we'll see how well they answer. (*Whisper the following instruction*) Let's tell them He is risen. Together now, "He is risen!" (*Congregation responds.*)

Regularly Refreshed

EASTER 2: Acts 3:13–15, 17–26; 1 John 5:1–6; John 20:19–31

Text. You killed the author of life, but God raised Him from the dead. We are witnesses of this. Repent, then, and turn to God, so that your sins may be wiped out, that times of refreshing may come from the Lord, and that He may send the Christ, who has been appointed for you—even Jesus. *Acts 3:15, 19–20*

Teaching aid. Can of wasp or insect-spray killer.

Gospel nugget. The living Lord, Jesus, wipes out our sins and refreshes us.

I saw a wasp in my house last week. First it was buzzing around by the windows. Then it would swoop down closer to the floor and zip into and out of all the rooms. The wasp frightened me because I didn't want to get stung. At first I thought I could kill the wasp with a rolled-up newspaper, but if I missed it on the first try, it might attack me. Then I remembered this can of insect killer. I waited until the wasp rested on the window sill, took aim, and sprayed the wasp. Just a small amount of this bug killer wiped out that wasp right away.

Sins are like wasps in some ways. Sins sting people. Sometimes our sins sting other people. If we're mean to brothers, sisters, or friends, we will hurt their feelings. Our mean behavior may feel like a wasp sting to them. We may sting others with sins when we refuse to share toys or when we complain about the food served at home.

Sins always sting the sinner, too. Have you ever been caught doing something naughty? How did you feel when you were caught? Getting caught makes us feel guilty and unhappy. Even if we seem to get away with naughty behavior, sometimes we get a guilty conscience, which makes us feel bad. And, if we get grounded or spanked, that stings a lot. The worst sting of sin is death. Sins are like wasps.

All our sins stung Jesus. Listen to these Bible words from Acts (*read text*). Did those words sting your ears? The Bible says that we killed Jesus with our sins. How horrible! Thank God that He has good news for us, too. God is willing to forgive us—to wipe out our sins. He invites us to repent.

Do you know how to repent? Thank God again! He makes it easy to repent. Step 1 is to bring our sins to Jesus, not to try to hide them from Him. Step 2 is asking Jesus to forgive us and believing that He saved us from our sins. Just like that (*snap your fingers*), God aims at our sins and wipes them out. He takes away from us the sting of death.

I've mentioned forgiveness many times today. What good is forgiveness? We know forgiveness makes us better. It's the only thing that keeps us in God's family. And forgiveness also changes the way we act. We don't want to sting Jesus with more sins. Instead we want to be more like Him. He loved God the heavenly Father, and He loved all people. That's the kind of life we forgiven sinners want to lead. Since we're not perfect as Jesus was, we often do not act like Him. When that happens, Jesus again takes aim at our sins (*demonstrate with can, but do not spray*) and wipes them out.

How often do we need our sins wiped out? Since we sin every day, we need to repent every day. You know, if I had a lot of wasps in my house every day, I would soon run out of this bug spray (*indicate can*). I would need to buy more cans at the store to keep up with the problem. But do we ever run out of forgiveness from Jesus? Of course not. Best of all, we don't need to buy forgiveness. It's free.

Prayer. Dear Jesus, thank You for helping us repent every day for wiping out our sins. Help us to follow You by behaving like You did when You lived here on earth. We want to live with You in heaven. Amen.

Nothing Better

EASTER 3: Acts 4:8–12; 1 John 1:1–2:2; Luke 24:36–49

Text. Salvation is found in no one else, for there is no other name under heaven given to men by which we must be saved. *Acts 4:12*

Teaching aid. Cardboard "treasure" box containing the following items: watch, shoe, stuffed toy, small mirror, and cross or small illustration of Jesus. Shield contents from children's view.

Gospel nugget. God provided Jesus Christ as the only means of salvation.

Welcome children. Today I brought a treasure box. I have several treasures inside to show you. When we have seen all the items, perhaps you can tell me which treasure is most important.

Let's look at the first item (*watch*). You probably know that people usually wrap this little clock around their arm. Tell me, what good is a wrist watch? People always want to know the time—time to wake up, time for bed, time for supper, time to go to the dentist, time for Sunday school. We're expected to do everything on time, so knowing the time is very important. Can knowing the time take away our sins? Of course not. But we know the time is coming when Jesus will take all believers to heaven. We'll want to be ready for that time.

Next, What is this? (*Hold up shoe.*) One used shoe. What good are shoes? Without them, our feet might get hurt. Stores sell many different kinds of shoes. They have walking shoes, dress shoes, running shoes, basketball shoes, tennis shoes, and shoes for just about everything else. Do you think anyone sells shoes for climbing up to heaven? Nobody could make shoes for that.

You'll like my next object (*stuffed toy*). Do any of you have stuffed toys? Sometimes we really love our stuffed toys. We can hug them and make believe they're alive. Sometimes we like to sleep with them because they make us feel safe and happy. Stuffed toys are great. But they're not real, are they? If you were sick, they might be nice to hold close, but they couldn't take your sickness away. Maybe you can count on stuffed toys to always be your friend, but there are times when you can't have your favorite stuffed toy with you. But one real Friend is always with you—your Friend Jesus.

Only two treasures left in the box. Look at this (*reveal mirror*). It's looking back at you. Have you ever played in front of a mirror? What did you do? (*Encourage responses.*) Making faces or just looking at yourself can be fun. Who wants to try looking like a scary monster? (*Allow volunteer to view self.*) Who wants to be a silly clown? (*Allow volunteer to view self.*) I'll show each of you who Jesus loves (*show each child self in mirror*).

Speaking of Jesus, here is something that reminds us of Him (*cross or illustration of Jesus*). Which of all these things is the most important treasure? You're right. The cross (illustration), because He is the only one who could save us. Watches, shoes, stuffed toys, mirrors, and all the other wonderful things in the world aren't nearly as important as Jesus. He is the most important treasure ever.

Prayer. Lord Jesus, thank You for blessing us with all the things we enjoy. We praise You for Your love and kindness. Help us always to remember that You are the most important treasure. In Your name we pray. Amen.

Always a Winner

EASTER 4: Acts 4:23–33; 1 John 3:1–2; John 10:11–18

Text. After they prayed, the place where they were meeting was shaken. And they were all filled with the Holy Spirit and spoke the word of God boldly. *Acts 4:31*

Teaching aid. Baseball bat.

Gospel nugget. For Jesus' sake, God answers prayers to His glory and for the good of His people.

When basketball, baseball, or football teams are very good, you might hear the players shouting, (*hold up bat*) "We're number one. We're number one." Today I brought along this baseball bat because it reminds me of the numeral one (*sweep fingers along length of bat to demonstrate*) and also because baseball season is just beginning. I wonder which team will win enough games to become the champion of the whole world. Do you have a favorite team? (*Invite responses.*)

The leader of a baseball team is called a manager. The players ask the manager questions, and the manager tells the players how best to play the game. Players really count on the manager to give them good advice. For example, when it was my turn to bat, I might want to swing hard so I could get the best hit of all, a home run. The fans would cheer, and I could dance around the bases waving my finger and shouting, "I'm number one. I'm number one." Of course, I might swing so hard that I would miss the ball completely.

The manager might have an idea that's better for the whole team. He might want me to bunt (*demonstrate*) so the ball just drops off the bat and surprises the other team. I might have a better chance of getting to first base with a little bunt than with a big swing. What I would do is up to the manager.

You and I are Christians, and Christians are like a team in some ways. I think you can guess our manager's name. (*Pause for responses.*) Yes, God is our manager. Can you also guess how we talk to God? We speak with God in our prayers. He answers our prayers, too. He speaks to us in the words of the Bible, and His Holy Spirit leads us to what is good. Many times we don't even know that God is leading us, but we can always trust Him because He knows just what we need.

God gave us many ways to talk to Him. What prayers do you know? Sometimes you talk to God when you say, "Come, Lord Jesus, be our guest . . . " or you might pray the Lord's Prayer, "Our Father in heaven . . . " At bedtime, perhaps you talk to God by saying, "Now I lay me down to sleep . . . " Have you ever talked to God with your own words? God hears those prayers, too.

We can pray any time. God is always ready to listen. And He always wants us to be winners. That's why He answers prayers in ways that are best for us. When I was your age, I wanted to be a _____ . Maybe I even prayed to be a _____ . God did what was best for Him and for me. I grew up to be a _____ . I'm glad He made me what I am. God answers all prayer that way. Sometimes we don't get exactly what we want, but He always gives us what is good.

God is powerful. He makes us winners each time we pray. Jesus' disciples certainly found out what God can do when we pray. Listen (*read text.*) God shows just how powerful He is when we pray for forgiveness. Through Jesus He destroys all our sins, and we win against the devil. God is generous, too. He gives us what we need to live. God certainly is a good manager. Let's thank Him for making us winners.

Prayer. Dear God, You know just what we need to be winners. That's why You sent Jesus to take away our sins. That's why You take care of us each day. We praise You dear Lord. You're number one for us. In Jesus' name we pray. Amen.

Welcome Words

EASTER 5: Acts 8:26–40; 1 John 3:18–24; John 15:1–8

Text. Then Philip began with that very passage of Scripture and told him the good news about Jesus. *Acts 8:35*

Teaching aid. Poster board on which is printed "Yahweh is the benevolent and supernatural divinity whose penchant for acts of agape transcends human cognitive ability." A second poster on which is printed "Jesus loves you very much."

Gospel nugget. The Holy Spirit reveals Jesus' love to people.

Here is an important message for God's children. (*Hold up first poster.*) Usually I ask one of you to read, but the words are quite large. Will it be okay if I read it for you? (*Read poster.*) Did you understand what I read? Probably not, and you're not alone. Long ago, in the days after the first Easter, a man read a message that he didn't understand. This man worked for the Queen of Ethiopia. (Ethiopia is a country in Africa.) He was reading some of Isaiah's words from the Bible, but he didn't understand what they meant. The Holy Spirit knew about the man's trouble, so He sent another man named Philip to explain Isaiah's words.

Philip's job was not easy. You see, the man from Ethiopia was riding in a special wagon called a chariot. Strong horses pulled chariots. We can imagine that the Ethiopian was rolling speedily down the road. Philip had to run along next to the chariot. He must have been out of breath when he shouted to the Ethiopian, "Do you understand what you are reading?"

The man answered, "How can I unless someone explains it to me?" With that, he invited Philip to ride with him in the chariot. As they rumbled down the road, Philip explained how much God loves people. He told the Ethiopian that God sent His Son Jesus to take away sins. The Ethiopian was excited about this good news. He believed what Philip told him. As the chariot passed near some water, the Ethiopian asked Philip to baptize him. So Philip baptized him, and the man became a Christian.

Good story, wasn't it? Do you remember this poster (*indicate poster*) filled with big words? You would need to attend school for many years before you could read and understand all these difficult words. But the Holy Spirit makes it easy to know what is most important. He puts the Good News in words most people can read and almost everyone can understand. Who will read this? (*Show second poster.*) Yes, Jesus loves you very much. He loves you so much that He suffered and died to take away your sins. That's a great reason for coming to church and Sunday school.

Do you ever get tired of hearing someone say, "I love you"? We always welcome those wonderful words. Jesus says those words every week in church and Sunday school. We hear how much God loves us when the pastor speaks. We thank God for loving us in the words that we pray. And when the church service ends, the pastor blesses us in God's name—another way of telling us that God loves us.

Do you go to Sunday school? Your Sunday school teachers are like Philip in some ways. They tell you what it says in the Bible. (*Sometimes they may even huff and puff to keep up with you.*) They know at least 52 ways to tell you how much Jesus loves you. Each week they tell Bible stories about how God takes care of His people. I hope you want to come back every Sunday to hear more stories about Jesus.

Let's read these Good News words one more time. All together now (*lead children*), "Jesus loves you very much."

Prayer. Thank You, Lord, for speeding Philip to the Ethiopian. Thank You also for sending pastors and Sunday school teachers to us. We want to hear how much You love us, too. Amen.

Evidence

EASTER 6: Acts 11:19–30; 1 John 4:1–11; John 15:9–17

Text. When he arrived and saw the evidence of the grace of God, he was glad and encouraged them all to remain true to the Lord with all their hearts. *Acts 11:23*

Teaching aid. Sets of related objects such as the following: thermometer, container of pain-relief or popular cough medicine, and small bandages; hammer, nails, and scraps of wood; bucket, cloth, cleaning powder or liquid; pot, pan, and mixing spoon; Bible, offering basket, and hymnbook.

Gospel nugget. God fills His people with grace so that others may know of His love.

Since today's Bible reading says that Barnabas saw evidence of God's grace, I thought we'd play a guessing game called "evidence." Evidence is a clue about something. Let's see how good you are with evidence.

Here are the first three clues—a thermometer, a container of pills, and some bandages. Evidence! Who might have left these objects behind? Yes, these are clues a doctor or nurse might leave behind.

Here is more evidence—a hammer, nails, and some wood. Who would use these things? Yes, a builder might use these to make a bench or to repair a hole in a roof.

More clues coming up—one bucket with a cloth and cleaning powder. What good are these things? They are used for cleaning—evidence that one of our "cleaner-uppers" was here making the church look beautiful.

Here's another clue. I found a pot, a pan, and a mixing spoon.

What kind of evidence is this? Someone who likes to cook left these clues.

Now I have one last question about evidence. Who would you find using a Bible, an offering basket, and a hymnbook? You and I use these. This evidence tells others that God gives us what we need to praise Him and serve others.

What is the Bible? The Bible speaks God's word. It tells us how Jesus died to take away our sins and how He rose again on Easter. In the Bible God promises that Jesus will come again so we can live with Him and our families in heaven. It tells us how to live happily and peacefully. But where did this Bible come from? Yes, God gave it to us.

What do we collect with this (*indicate offering basket*)? We use these every Sunday to collect money. Did you ever wonder where that money goes? (*Invite answers and expect some surprises. Then share how your church uses the offerings.*) Offering baskets have been around ever since the very first Christians met together to worship Jesus. Today's Bible reading told how some disciples took an offering to help other Christians who couldn't grow their own food because of bad weather. We use offering baskets to share with others what God gives us. Even though the money you give probably comes from Mom or Dad, who worked to earn it, that money is a sign—evidence—that God has blessed you. It's good to give some back to God so others can hear about His love, too.

Our last evidence is this hymnbook. It contains songs about Jesus. Some people sing when they're happy, others sing when they're sad or frightened, and still others sing as a way of praying.

You yourselves are evidence that Jesus loves you. You're here with all these other Christians to pray, sing, and hear about Jesus. I'm glad we're together this morning. Let's pray that Jesus will always keep us together.

Prayer. Dear Lord Jesus, thank You for making us Christian. Thanks for all the evidence that You love us. Help us to tell and show others clues about Your love. In Your name we pray. Amen.

What's Inside?

EASTER 7: Acts 1:15–26; 1 John 4:13–21; John 17:11b–19

Text. Then they prayed, "Lord, You know everyone's heart." *Acts 1:24a*

Teaching aid. A cardboard box with several nuts, bolts, screws, nails, or washers sealed inside.

Gospel nugget. The Holy Spirit places faith in the hearts of believers.

Would you like to see what is in this box? I would, too. But the box is taped shut. Maybe we can guess what is inside by the size of the box. What could fit in here? (*Encourage speculation.*) Those are good guesses. Perhaps we should try to guess what's inside by the way the box smells. Could a skunk be inside this box? How about a bottle of perfume? We can't smell anything, can we?

Do you have any other suggestions how we might guess what is inside without opening the box? Let's try shaking it. Oh, it rattles. What does it sound like?

We can't know what is really in the box unless we actually look inside. But we can't look inside because the box is sealed. We will keep it sealed for a while yet. Right now, I would like to read a Bible passage to you. (*Read text—Acts 1:24a.*)

It sounds a little as if the Lord is a heart doctor. What do heart doctors do? Yes, heart doctors take care of people with sick hearts. They take special pictures of a person's heart to see if it's working correctly. If the heart is sick, heart doctors might give a person special medicine or other treatments to help the sick heart get better. Why is a healthy heart important? Yes, people need healthy hearts to live.

Jesus looks at our hearts to see if they are filled with faith. He wants to know if we believe that He took away our sins. Jesus wants to know if we're ready to share the love in our hearts with other people.

Jesus often sees hearts that are sick with sin. Sin-sick hearts belong to people who refuse to say they are sorry for not living the way Jesus wants them to live. Sin-sick hearts don't want to share or be kind. Sin-sick hearts belong to people who say bad words or hurt other people. Are your hearts ever sick with sin? We all have sin-sick hearts. That's why we need Doctor Jesus.

Jesus keeps our hearts clean and healthy. He looks inside us and says, "Hey, you need some help, and I've got it for you." So Jesus gives us some medicine. What do you suppose that medicine is? It's forgiveness. What wonderful medicine! We don't have to swallow it or taste it. Jesus just gives it to us, and it takes away our sins. His medicine makes us healthy enough to do good things for others.

Jesus always knows what's inside our hearts. When we do something wrong or bad, we don't need to say, "I didn't do it!" We can say to Jesus, "I'm sorry I acted badly. Please forgive me." Jesus likes to hear those words, "I'm sorry." His whole job while He was on earth was to be perfect for us and to die for the wrong things we do. Because Jesus heals our sin-sick hearts, we will live forever.

Now back to the box. Let's open it. (*Open box.*) Well, who would have guessed that we had nuts, bolts, screws, and washers inside? You can never tell what might be in a closed-up box. But Jesus always knows what's in our closed-up hearts. He keeps taking out our sin and putting in faith and forgiveness in its place.

Prayer. Dear Doctor Jesus, keep our hearts healthy and free from sin. Help other people to know that You died to take away their sins, too. Amen.

Bubble and Fizz

PENTECOST: Ezek. 37:1–14; Acts 2:22–36; John 7:37–39a

Text. I will put my Spirit in you and you will live, and I will settle you in your own land. Then you will know that I the LORD have spoken, and I have done it, declares the LORD. *Ezek. 37:14*

Teaching aid. An Alka-Seltzer or similar tablet and a clear glass filled with water.

Gospel nugget. God sends the Holy Spirit, who gives us new life in Christ.

Look here. I've got this huge tablet that will do something special for us. (*Set tablet down in front of children, but not in the water.*) Watch it closely now. (*Pause.*) I don't know what's wrong. I was told this tablet would bubble with life, but it's just sitting there peacefully. Perhaps if I drop it in a glass of water something will happen. (*Place tablet in water.*) Look at that! It's fizzing away. See the bubbles. It almost looks alive.

This fizzing tablet reminds me of a story from the Bible book of Ezekiel. Did you hear it awhile ago? It is a story about bones. Let me give you a little rerun of that story.

Ezekiel worked for God. One day, God took him out to a valley and showed him an awful sight. The ground was littered with dried-up old bones. God told Ezekiel that the bones belonged to His people. What horrible news! God's people appeared to be dead, nothing left but bones. But God said He would breathe on the bones. God told Ezekiel to talk to the bones and, as Ezekiel talked to the bones, a miracle happened. The bones got up and took on muscles and flesh and formed into new human bodies. They came to life with special breath that God gave them. Why would God do such a strange miracle? The Bible tells us. Listen. (*Read Ezek. 37:14*).

God said, "I will put my spirit in you, and you will live." He showed His love and power to Ezekiel. God wanted His people to live new lives for Him. Many years later, on a day called Pentecost, God gave new life to some other people.

A crowd of Jesus' followers gathered in a small room. God sent His Spirit to them in another miracle. Little patches like fire danced above the people's heads, and they heard what sounded like a loud rushing wind. That wind and fire were signs that the Holy Spirit was giving new life to Jesus' followers. When it was all over, they rushed out to tell others about Jesus' love.

Many, many years after the first Pentecost, God gave you a miracle. He gave you new life. I'm not talking about the day you were born to your mom and dad. I'm talking about the day you became a Christian. People who aren't Christians are like dead old bones in the desert. They just lie there and do nothing. They have no life. But when God breathed His Holy Spirit on you, you came alive. You bubbled and fizzed because the Holy Spirit filled you with Jesus' love and forgiveness. Best of all, He gave You love and forgiveness for free. It's as if God looked down from heaven at you and said, "That's one of my kids! I love you. I want you to have my Spirit." Now you have power to serve God by what you do for other people. You have power because Jesus bubbles and fizzes inside you.

Bow your heads and fold your hands now. Take this blessing from the Lord.

Prayer. Dear Holy Spirit, make these children bubble with Your love and fizz that love on everyone they meet. For Jesus' sake. Amen.

Three Names in One

HOLY TRINITY: Deut. 6:4–9; Rom. 8:14–17; John 3:1–17

Text. Hear, O Israel: The LORD our God, the LORD is one. *Deut. 6:4*

Teaching aid. Three index cards. On one print FATHER; on one, JESUS; and on one, HOLY SPIRIT. Print GOD on a sack in which the three cards will fit.

Gospel nugget. All three persons of the Trinity accomplish their saving work because they are one God.

If you have listened carefully in church and Sunday school, you probably noticed something strange about how we talk about God. Sometimes we call God Father (*show card*); sometimes we call Him Jesus, the Son (*show card*); and sometimes we call God the Holy Spirit (*show card*). Although we may call God by three different names, they are all names for the one true God. (*Place cards in sack marked GOD as you are speaking.*)

I want you to know about God's different names. (*Remove "Father" from sack.*) God is our heavenly Father. We call Him our Father because He gives us the whole world and everything in it. Maybe you know how God created the earth, sea, sky, plants, and animals just by saying a few words. Best of all, He made Adam and Adam's wife, Eve. They had no Mom and Dad as we do. God made them to be His very own children. God loved all that He created, but He loved Adam and Eve best. They were in charge of everything that God made. And when Adam and Eve disobeyed God, He promised to keep on loving them anyway.

We are God's children, too. He made us His own daughters and sons when He gave us faith. Although we also disobey God, He keeps on loving us anyway.

God the Father always loves us because of (*remove card from sack*) Jesus, God's Son. God has many laws for all of us to obey. He wants everyone to praise Him and to get along with one another. God says, "Obey all My laws, be perfect." But nobody can obey all the laws. We all need help getting to heaven. That's where Jesus comes in. God said to all people, "Since you can't obey Me, I'll send Jesus to obey Me for you. Then you can be sure that you'll get to go to heaven."

The Bible says Jesus is true God and also a human being like you and me. He did everything right. He never did wrong. He got hurt and finally He died for our sins. Best of all, Jesus rose from the dead. We'll be with Him in heaven someday.

Finally, we know God as the Holy Spirit (*remove card from sack*). God the Holy Spirit has had some important jobs. Do you know what the Holy Spirit did when Jesus was baptized? He came down like a dove. And the Holy Spirit, like wind or small flames of fire, filled Jesus' friends on the first Pentecost. But the Holy Spirit didn't stop there. He comes into the heart of every Christian who ever lived. That includes you and me. God the Holy Spirit has made us Christians. In fact, the Holy Spirit is very busy right here this morning. He is building our faith as we share God's Word. The Holy Spirit even prays for us!

We call God the Triune God. Triune is a special word which means three persons (*return cards to sack, one by one*) but only one true God (*hold up sack*). When we talk to God, we can call Him by any of His names. God will listen. He knows who we are because He made us His own children through Jesus, and His Holy Spirit is always with us.

Prayer. Dear God, thank You for making us Your own children. Dear Holy Jesus, thank You for taking away our sins. Dear Holy Spirit, thank You for keeping us close to You. Amen.

Take a Rest

PENTECOST 2: Deut. 5:12–15; 2 Cor. 4:5–12; Mark 2:23–28

Text. But the seventh day is a Sabbath to the Lord your God. *Deut. 5:14a*

Teaching aid. A bed pillow.

Gospel nugget. We have true rest because Jesus saved us.

I brought my pillow today because we're going to talk about God's Third Commandment. Do any of you know it? The Third Commandment goes like this. "Remember the Sabbath Day by keeping it holy." *Sabbath* means "rest day," "Remember the rest day by keeping it holy." God wants His people to have a rest day, and to keep it special.

Today is our Sabbath. That's why I brought my pillow. People rest on pillows, right? But I must be careful not to rest so well that I fall asleep. So let's think how we can make our rest day special.

God wants us to worship on our rest day. That's why we're in church. We pray, we say we're sorry for our sins and receive forgiveness, we give our offerings to God, and we sing. Do you have any favorite "Jesus songs"? (*Allow children to suggest several. Choose one familiar to both children and older people, if possible, and sing it a cappella.*) How good it is to sing Jesus songs and rest at the same time!

Praying together is another way to make the Sabbath Day special or holy. Do you have a favorite prayer? (*Encourage responses. Choose a familiar prayer and invite the children and congregation to join in prayer.*) We certainly feel rested when we know that Jesus hears our prayer and that we can trust Him to do what is best for us.

We Christians also gather on the Sabbath Day to hear God forgive our sins. We know Jesus died for our sins long ago. But each Sabbath Day is a good time to confess our sins to God. Confessing means telling God that we know we haven't been perfect, and that we need His forgiveness. Let's confess our sins right now. Repeat after me.

Dear God (*allow time for children to repeat phrases*) . . . I know that I haven't always obeyed you . . . Sometimes I'm unkind to others . . . Sometimes I won't listen to my parents . . . Sometimes I forget to pray . . . Sometimes I don't feel like coming to church . . . And sometimes I don't even know that I'm sinning . . . Forgive me . . . for Jesus' sake.

Thinking about all our sins, we might not feel happy or well rested. But listen to this. "In the name and for the sake of Jesus Christ, God forgives all your sins!" We don't have to worry about our sins when we give them to Jesus. Jesus takes them away and God forgives them. We can rest knowing that God won't let our sins hurt us or trap us.

Part of our Sabbath worship includes offerings. Many people give money offerings because they're thankful for God's blessings. People also give other offerings to God. When the church choir sings, they offer their voices in praise to God. Sunday school teachers offer their time to teach girls and boys more about Jesus. You give God an offering each time you help someone. Whatever you give to God is your offering.

For a day of rest the Sabbath Day certainly seems busy. Have you ever cuddled up to Mom or Dad and fallen asleep after a busy day? We can feel that way after worshiping God, too. We can rest on Jesus. He will always love us.

Prayer. Dear God, thank You for leading us to worship You. Make our days of rest happy times for praying, singing, and giving our best to You. In Jesus' name. Amen.

*C*over-up

PENTECOST 3: Gen. 3:9–15; 2 Cor. 4:13–18; Mark 3:20–35

Text. And I will put enmity between you and the woman, and between your offspring and hers; he will crush your head, and you will strike his heel. *Gen. 3:15*

Teaching aid. A cookie and a small throw rug or carpet square.

Gospel nugget. Jesus covered our sins through His death and resurrection.

Did you ever get in big trouble because you did something wrong? Have you ever used excuses like "Who me?" or "It wasn't my fault, he did it first"? I'd like to tell you a story about a boy named Monte who got into big trouble.

It started with a cookie like this (*show cookie*). Monte was hungry. He asked Mom for some cookies. But she said, "It's only a half hour until lunchtime. No cookies until after we eat."

Now Monte was disappointed and hungry. He whined and complained a little, but Mom just ignored him. Then Mom went outside to wash her car. The kitchen was empty. Monte thought about how much he really wanted a cookie. He got a great idea when he saw the stool by the bathroom sink. If he stood on the stool, he could reach the cookie box in the cabinet. Mom would never know if a few cookies were missing. Monte climbed on the stool, opened the cabinet door, and saw the cookie box behind the jar of peanuts. Monte pushed the peanut jar out of the way—way out of the way, right off the shelf and onto the floor, where the jar top popped open. Peanuts scattered in all directions. While Monte was stepping down from the stool, he accidentally grabbed the top of the cookie box. Suddenly it was raining cookies! Monte quickly put the stool away. He picked up the peanuts and threw them in the garbage. He threw several cookies in the garbage, too. Two cookies were left to clean up. He stuck one in his mouth, but before he could finish chewing, his mom came in the front door. Monte took the rug (*demonstrate*) and placed it over the one remaining cookie. Monte was pretty sure that he had covered up his wrongdoing.

Maybe it was the crumbs on his lips or the lump under the rug that gave Monte's sin away. Mom asked him about the cookies. Monte started to say, "Well, Mom, YOU wouldn't let me have anything to eat, and I was starving to death, and all the kids in the world get to eat cookies when they want to, and, and, and . . . " and Monte ran out of excuses. So he started again. "Mom, I'm sorry I disobeyed you. I guess I'll have to do without cookies for the rest of my life." Then Mom surprised Monte. She said, "Yes, Monte, you disobeyed me. It will be awhile before I'll buy cookies. But I also forgive you. You may have cookies again next week."

Most grown-ups know how Monte felt. The very first grown-ups, Adam and Eve, knew what it was like to be in big trouble. And they made excuses, too. God made a home for Adam and Eve and all the animals in a beautiful garden. He gave them many interesting fruits and vegetables to eat. The only fruit God said they couldn't eat came from a tree that would hurt Adam and Eve.

One day the devil, disguised as a friendly snake, tempted Eve to eat the fruit from that tree. She gave in and ate it. Adam ate some, too. As soon as they ate that fruit, they knew they had disobeyed God. They felt guilty and ashamed. Adam blamed Eve for disobeying, and Eve blamed the snake. Adam and Eve tried to cover up their sins. But God saw under the covers.

We don't need to cover up our sins. Jesus takes them away. He buries our sins so that God will never see them again. Jesus covers up our sins each time we ask Him to forgive us. Let's make Jesus happy by living according to His rules. But always remember that He's ready to cover up our sins whenever we fail.

Starting Over

PENTECOST 4: Ezek. 17:22–24; 2 Cor. 5:1–10; Mark 4:26–34

Text. All the trees of the field will know that I the LORD bring down the tall tree and make the low tree grow tall. I dry up the green tree and make the dry tree flourish. I the LORD have spoken, and I will do it. *Ezek. 17:24*

Teaching aid. Several sheets of paper crumpled into a ball and two flat sheets.

Gospel nugget. God in His love sent the Savior because people cannot save themselves.

My friend Renee gave me these wads of paper. Renee was writing a letter to her grandpa. She had lots of trouble writing what she wanted to say, and she made many mistakes. Every time Renee made a mistake she got disgusted, crinkled up her paper (*demonstrate*), and tossed it aside. Soon she had so many balls of paper that her bedroom looked as if a herd of snowballs had attacked it. But Renee was patient. She kept starting over until she was happy with Grandpa's letter.

God would understand Renee's problem. He wants all people to be saved from sin to live in heaven. But people mess up His plans.

First, Adam and Eve wanted more. God gave them everything possible to make them happy in the Garden of Eden. Yet they disobeyed God and became the first sinners on earth. God still loved them even after they disobeyed Him. He gave Adam and Eve two sons. It should have been a happy family. But one of the boys killed his brother. More unhappiness! Things got worse and worse until God became very angry because people were messing up His plans. So God sent a flood to wash away the mess.

Even during the flood, God showed how much He loved people. He saved Noah and his family along with many animals. For God, it was like starting over, crumpling up the world (*crumple second sheet of paper*) and giving it a fresh start with some people who believed in Him.

The world wasn't perfect after Noah and the ark found dry land. The sons and daughters of Noah's family often forgot God. They did things that made God angry. Many people fell away from God completely and didn't know Him at all. So God decided to choose a certain group of people to be His children. They were called the children of Israel.

God made a special promise to the children of Israel. He promised always to be with them. Wow! What love. Can you guess what happened? Many of the children of Israel forgot God. But God never forgot them. He even promised to send the whole world a Savior, since nobody could stop messing up His plan. At last Jesus came to die and take away the world's sins.

You're God's children now. I'm a bit older, but I'm God's child, too. And you know what? I'm not perfect. I sometimes disobey God. I think you disobey Him sometimes too. But God always forgives us and allows us to start over. Since people can't be good enough for God all by themselves, He sent Jesus to start over, to make people good enough for God by taking away their sins. That's what Ezekiel is talking about in today's Bible reading. (*Read text.*)

We can start over each day. When you wake up each morning, there are many new things to play, see, and think about. Best of all, we can start every day knowing that Jesus makes us good enough for God.

Prayer. Dear Heavenly Father, thank You for letting us start over each time we mess up Your plans by disobeying You. Help us obey You by loving others and loving You most of all. In Jesus' name we pray. Amen.

Silly Questions

PENTECOST 5: Job 38:1–11; 2 Cor. 5:14–21; Mark 4:35–41

Text. Then the LORD answered Job out of the storm. He said: "Who is this that darkens my counsel with words without knowledge?" *Job 38:1–2*

Teaching aid. A large question mark drawn on a piece of cardboard.

Gospel nugget. God saved us with limitless power and wisdom beyond human comprehension.

What is this mark (*show question mark*)? When do we use question marks? Silly question, wasn't it? We use question marks when we write questions. Let's try a game. I need an assistant to hold up this question mark each time I ask a question. (*Choose an older child or an adult to assist.*)

Why did the chicken cross the road? To buy a rowboat. Silly question, wasn't it? The answer was even sillier. Here's another one, but it's a knock-knock joke so our question mark assistant must listen carefully to get the question mark in the right places.

Knock, knock. (*Encourage children to respond*) Who's there? Tuba. (*Children respond*) Tuba who? Tuba toothpaste. Now that was really a silly answer for a silly joke! (*Thank and relieve assistant.*)

Job was a man from the Bible who asked silly questions. It all began when he got mad at God. You see, Job's life was filled with trouble, unhappiness, disaster, sadness, fear, pain, sickness, and zillions of other things that could easily make anyone angry with God. Job blamed God for all the bad things that happened. Perhaps you can imagine how Job felt if you put on your "pretending hats."

Pretend that you just woke up. Go ahead, stretch and yawn. (*Demonstrate actions if you're comfortable doing so. Invite children to join you.*) You wobble over to your dresser drawers and pull out some clothes. You put on your shoes. Then you put on your socks. Oh, oh, you must be really tired! Your big brother comes by and laughs at the way you look. Then you go to the table for breakfast. You see a piece of burnt toast smeared with boysenberry jelly. You complain and Mom tells you that the poor people in China would be happy for such a breakfast. Now you're mad at Mom, AND you feel ashamed that you complained. You decide to play with your favorite puzzle. When you shake the box, the lid slips open and 200 puzzle pieces dance, prance, roll, and skip across the floor—199 pieces seem to end up right in the path of Mom's roaring vacuum cleaner. Whoosh. Only one piece left of your favorite puzzle. Mom says, "I told you to be more careful with that box." Your brother says, "Hey, small fry, having a bad morning? Maybe you should *pray* about it." What a silly thing to say! Besides you might say something silly to God like, "Hey God, You got something against me today?" Silly question.

God wants only good things for you. He always knows what's best for His people. Job had a miserable time because the devil was trying to take him away from God. Job did question God. He asked God, "Why are all these bad things happening to me?"

God answered, (*read text*). What God meant is this: "Silly question. Don't you think I know what's best? I was smart enough and powerful enough to create the whole world. I think I'm smart enough and powerful enough to do some good for you. Wait. Be patient. I'll take care of you."

Job did wait, and God stayed close to him. Finally God chased the devil away from Job and made him happier than he ever was before. Because Jesus is our Savior, God will do the same for us. So the next time you're having a bad day, maybe you should pray about it.

Let's practice. Repeat after me: "Dear God . . . when I'm having a bad day . . . Please make me happy again . . . I'll wait for Your help . . . Amen.

God's Guarantee

PENTECOST 6: Lam. 3:22–33;
2 Cor. 8:1–9, 13–14; Mark 5:21–24a, 35–43
or Mark 5:24b–34

Text. Because of the LORD's great love we are not consumed, for his compassions never fail. They are new every morning; great is your faithfulness. *Lam. 3:22-23*

Teaching aid. Wristwatch.

Gospel nugget. God's grace is guaranteed to last an eternal lifetime.

How do you like my wristwatch? (*Show watch.*) I really like it, too. This watch is guaranteed to last a long time. Do you know what *guaranteed* means? The people who made this watch promise that it won't fall apart and that it will tell the right time.

God also has made many guarantees, or promises. We can't talk about all of them, but let me tell you some of His guarantees.

Here is a great guarantee from God: "Call upon Me in the day of trouble; I will deliver you, and you will honor Me" (Ps. 50:15). What kind of troubles can we tell God? He wants us to pray about everything. If we are sick, ask Him for better health. If we just had a fight with our best friend, ask His forgiveness and His help to become friends again. When we are afraid of the dark or of a thunderstorm, ask for protection. And what does God guarantee? He says, "I will deliver you." That means God will hear our prayers and that He will help in a way that's best for us. That's God's own guarantee!

Here is another guarantee from God. "He will command His

angels concerning you to guard you in all your ways" (Ps. 91:11). Now there's a guarantee nobody but God could make. God promises help from angels. You can't see angels, but if God says they are protecting you, you can trust that He's not lying. God's angels know you, and they will always do what's best for you, too.

Now for another Bible passage about God's guarantees. "For I am convinced that neither death nor life, neither angels nor demons, neither the present nor the future, nor any powers, neither height nor depth, nor anything else in all creation, will be able to separate us from the love of God that is in Christ Jesus our Lord" (Rom. 8:38–39). Because Jesus died for you, nothing can keep you from having God's love. Even the devil himself can't stop God from loving you. God guarantees that you belong to Him.

God has made such wonderful guarantees. I can share only one more. "For the Lord Himself will come down from heaven, . . . After that, we who are still alive and are left will be caught up together with them in the clouds to meet the Lord in the air. And so we will be with the Lord forever" (1 Thess. 4:16, 17).

When Jesus went up to heaven many, many years ago, some angels made this guarantee. They said Jesus will return some day. When He does, He'll take you and me and all Christians everywhere with Him to heaven. Once we're in heaven, we'll never die. We'll always be happy and safe. We'll actually see Jesus in person every day.

Aren't God's guarantees great? Today's Bible reading tells us one more thing about these guarantees. They will not quit or run out. Listen: "Because of the Lord's great love, . . . His compassions never fail. They are new every morning."

Let's thank God for His eternal, lifetime guarantees.

Prayer. Dear God, You are so good to us. Thank You for promising to protect us. Thank You for promising to take us to heaven. In Jesus' name we pray. Amen.

A Message for Sinners

PENTECOST 7: Ezek. 2:1–5; 2 Cor. 12:7–10; Mark 6:1–6

Text. He said: "Son of man, I am sending you to the Israelites, to a rebellious nation that has rebelled against me; they and their fathers have been in revolt against me to this very day." *Ezek. 2:3*

Teaching aid. A sealed envelope addressed to you, containing an advertisement; and a second sealed and addressed envelope (church stationery) containing this message "Sinner, repent and be saved."

Gospel nugget. God does not abandon His people even if they abandon Him.

Do you ever get letters or cards in the mail? I got these the other day, but I'm not sure I want them. I have three choices of what to do with this mail. I can toss it in the garbage can without looking at it. I can open the envelope, read what's inside, and then throw it away. Or I can open the envelope, read what's inside, and do what the letter asks me to do.

I think I will see what's inside (*open first envelope and remove contents*). It says that I can buy a magazine subscription to (*your favorite magazine*) for only half price. I'm glad I opened that envelope! Here is a second envelope. It's from our church. Should I open it or throw it out? I think I'll see what the church has to say.

The message says, "Sinner, repent and be saved." I'm not sure I like that message. Should I pitch it out or keep it? In today's Bible reading God tells Ezekiel, "I am sending you . . . to a rebellious nation." I guess God sometimes sends us messages we might not like to get, so I had better listen.

But I don't like being called a sinner, do you? If I'm a sinner that means I've done some things that God doesn't like. Really, I'm a very good person. Well, maybe not always. This morning I didn't want to come to church because I really wanted to sleep longer. Then I blamed someone else when I couldn't find my shoes. And I daydreamed instead of singing the first hymn. It's still early in the day, and I guess I have done a few things wrong. I really am a sinner. Maybe I should be thankful that the message says "sinner." That means it is for me. Jesus came to save sinners.

The message goes on to say, "Repent and be saved." That sounds too hard. Maybe I'll repent tomorrow. If I repent, I must say I'm sorry for doing wrong, for being a sinner. That's the easy part. The hard part of repenting is doing what God wants us to do.

How often do you think a person needs to repent? We need to repent as often as we do wrong. Can anyone go even one day without sinning? Of course, not. So we also need to repent each day.

Good thing God never runs out of forgiveness! Good thing Jesus died for those who don't always want to go to church or Sunday school. Hard as we try, we don't always obey our parents. Jesus comes for us, and for those who sometimes love their pets more than they love God. Jesus died for children who say mean things to their friends and for those who grumble and complain about everything *(take a deep breath)* and for those who lie about having their homework done and for those who watch TV shows they shouldn't be watching and for those who cheat at games and for those who . . . *(take another deep breath)* oh, the list could go on forever.

God sent Jesus to save sinners. So let's all of us sinners, young and old, repent. Let's repent right now. Repeat this prayer with me:

Prayer. Dear God . . . I am a sinner . . . in need of forgiveness . . . Thank You for sending Jesus . . . to save me . . . Help me to live better . . . Amen.

God forgives you! Go in peace.

You Have a Call

PENTECOST 8: Amos 7:10–15; Eph. 1:3–14; Mark 6:7–13

Text. But the Lord took me from tending the flock and said to me, "Go, prophesy to my people Israel." *Amos 7:15*

Teaching aid. Telephone.

Gospel nugget. God calls common people to declare the Gospel.

(*Walk to presentation area while pretending to talk on telephone. Hold the handset away from your mouth while calling children forward. Pretend to muffle mouthpiece as children gather.*)

Will you excuse me for a moment while I complete this conversation? (*Conduct imaginary conversation*) "Yes, I understand . . . Well, it's a bit unusual you know . . . Perhaps you should ask someone else to do this job . . . You really want me, huh? . . . Well, okay . . . Thank you for calling." (*Hang up.*)

Thanks for waiting so patiently. That was an important call, and I needed to finish it. Do you get many telephone calls? Has God ever called you?

God has called some people in strange ways. Earlier, you might have heard the name *Amos* mentioned in the Bible reading. God called Amos. Before Amos was Amos, a prophet, he was Amos, a gardener and shepherd. But God came to Amos and said, "I have a job for you. Go, tell my people they have forgotten about Me. Without Me on their side, they are headed for big trouble." Amos listened to God. He became a prophet who tried to remind people of everything God had to say.

The Holy Spirit still calls people today. The Holy Spirit works through your family, pastor, Sunday school teachers, and other people to give you a strong faith. You need to be strong because God is already calling you to work for Him.

The Bible tells why God is calling you. It says, "For we are God's workmanship, created in Christ Jesus to do good works, which God prepared in advance for us to do" (Eph. 2:10). God calls you and me to do good things for others. What good things can you do? (*Encourage responses.*) God called you to do all those good things. No matter how old you are, you can always do something good for others.

What do you want to be when you grow up? (*Remember as many responses as possible. Respond in ways similar to those that follow.*) Sometimes people think only pastors do God's work, but God calls all people to serve Him. If you wanted to be a nurse, how could you do God's work? Nurses do God's work when they help sick people get better.

How might truck drivers do God's work? Truck drivers are serving God when they drive safely and are honest. They may help other drivers whose cars break down on the highway.

Teachers do God's work, too. How can they do good for others? Teachers love the children in their classes and pray for them. Teachers do God's work when they forgive and correct those children who like to cause trouble and break school rules.

No matter what you want to be when you grow up, you can begin working for God now. Amos was still a boy when God called him. You can do good things for other people. When you're a (*mention some career ambitions expressed by children*) someday, you'll know how to do what God created you to do. The Holy Spirit will help you.

God calls you always to do your best. Work for God, whatever you do. He gave us His best when He sent Jesus to take away our sins. That was a job no one else could do. Jesus did the job perfectly, even though it was very difficult to take away everybody's sins. Let's thank God for Jesus' doing His job by doing our very best for Him.

The Shepherd's Umbrella

PENTECOST 9: Jer. 23:1–6; Eph. 2:13–22; Mark 6:30–34

Text. "I will place shepherds over them who will tend them, and they will no longer be afraid or terrified, nor will any be missing," declares the LORD. *Jer. 23:4*

Teaching aid. Umbrella.

Gospel nugget. The Lord sends "shepherds" in the name of the Shepherd to shelter His children.

Umbrellas have many good uses. (*Open umbrella.*) We use umbrellas most often so we won't get wet when it rains, or too hot in the sun. Can you think of any other uses? (*Demonstrate the following.*) I might use an umbrella to chase off a pesky dog nipping at my heels, or to balance myself on the high wire in a circus. Umbrellas make good pointers (*tap pew with umbrella*). An umbrella can even become a spinning top (hold it upside down and spin it on the floor). But as I said before, umbrellas most often shelter or protect us from rain or sun.

God is like an umbrella. He shelters us in many different ways. God shelters you by giving you a house to live in. Your house keeps you safe from the rain or hot sun or cold night air. Your house shelters you with walls and a roof to protect you from all sorts of harmful things. Our church is another shelter God gives us. It reminds us how God protects us from our worst enemy, the devil. (*Point to the lectern with umbrella.*) Do you see the Bible? The Bible tells us all that God does to protect us. Over there (*indicate baptismal font with umbrella*) is the baptismal font. That's where the Holy Spirit comes inside us to be our personal protector. At the altar (*indicate with umbrella*) we pray to God for help, and on Communion Sundays you'll see people come near the altar for the Lord's Supper. The Lord's Supper gives us forgiveness, and forgiveness protects people by keeping us close to God. And over there (*point to pastor with umbrella*) is the pastor.

(*Read text.*) Today's Bible reading from Jeremiah says that pastors are like umbrellas from God. It calls pastors *shepherds*. That's a pretty good name for pastors. In fact, Jesus called Himself a shepherd. Shepherds protect sheep the way umbrellas shelter us. Shepherds keep the sheep together in a bunch as much as possible. But sometimes sheep wander away. Then shepherds go looking until they find and rescue any lost sheep. Wild animals like wolves or mountain lions may want to attack and eat sheep. Shepherds protect their flocks by chasing away such enemies. They also lead their hungry sheep to find fresh grass.

Our pastor doesn't take care of sheep. Neither did Jesus. But they do shelter us, like umbrellas. Our church shepherds give us Jesus' words so we won't be afraid. Church shepherds feed us God's Word so we will be healthy Christians. They do that with Bible stories.

Parents are shepherds—and umbrellas—for Jesus, too. They guide you to Jesus by saying prayers with you, bringing you along to church and Sunday school, teaching you Jesus songs, and telling you Bible stories. You're like very special sheep to your shepherd parents because God gave you to them, and it's their job to tell you about Jesus' love.

Jesus was the best Shepherd of all. Thousands and thousands of people know how much He loves them. He even died to protect His people from their enemy, the devil. Let's thank Jesus for being our Shepherd and for sending other shepherds, like umbrellas, to shelter us.

Prayer. Dear Jesus, thank You for making us like Your sheep. We need Your protection, and we thank You for all those who lead us in Your name today. Help us to be shepherds for others, too. Amen.

Knowing God

PENTECOST 10: Ex. 24:3–11; Eph. 4:1–7, 11–16; John 6:1–15

Text. But God did not raise his hand against these leaders of the Israelites; they saw God, and they ate and drank. *Ex. 24:11*

Teaching aid. A red-letter Bible, an illustration of Jesus, and a paper sack large enough to fit over both.

Gospel nugget. We know God's love through Jesus Christ and the Bible.

Can any of you tell us what God is like? (*Encourage responses.*)

We aren't the only ones who wonder about God. Long ago, people thought they could know God better if they actually saw him. But even Moses, a hero of God's people, didn't get to see God. God told Moses, "You cannot see My face, for no one may see Me and live" (Ex. 33:20).

But God also wanted people to know Him even though they couldn't look at Him as He really is, so He came to people in some unusual ways. Once He was in a fiery bush that never burned up. Another time He was a loud voice coming from the sky. Today's lesson from the Old Testament tells about a special way God showed himself to Moses, Aaron, and some other people. They saw God standing on a floor made of clear, bright sapphire jewels.

None of us has seen God in these ways. Maybe it's hard to imagine what God is like since we haven't seen Him. But under this sack, I have two things that help us know God. (*Remove sack.*)

(*Indicate illustration of Jesus.*) The first way we get to know

God is through this person. Do you know Him? Of course, it's Jesus.

Many years ago, people actually met Jesus. They talked to Him just as we're talking now. Can you imagine sitting here and actually talking with Jesus our Savior? God sent His Son to earth to show us what He is like. Jesus was a real person like you, and at the same time He was really God.

After Jesus lived on earth, He went to heaven. Right now we don't have a chance to hear Him speak in person. But in a way, we can hear Jesus' words. The Bible (*indicate Bible*) is also called the Word of God. It contains everything God wants us to know about Him. The Bible even tells what Jesus said. This Bible (*open to red-letter verses*) has Jesus' words in red.

(*Consider reading the texts below directly from the Bible.*) I thought of some things that I'd like to know about God. The Bible helped me. For example, how can we be sure that Jesus really wants us to love all people? The Bible says, "But I tell you who hear Me: Love your enemies, do good to those who hate you, bless those who curse you, pray for those who mistreat you" (Luke 6:27–28). Those words are Jesus' voice.

How do we know that God loves children? Here's what Jesus says in the Bible: (*Consider using the bracketed words to simplify the text.*) "People were bringing little children to Jesus to have him touch them, but the disciples rebuked [scolded] them. When Jesus saw this, he was indignant [angry]. He said to them, "Let the little children come to Me, and do not hinder [stop] them, for the kingdom of God belongs to such as these" (Mark 10:13–14). We know God loves children because Jesus loved children.

How can we believe that Jesus came to save people? We have Jesus' very own words in the Bible. Jesus said . . . "It is not the healthy who need a doctor, but the sick. I have not come to call the righteous, but sinners" (Matt. 9:12–13).

We know that God is our friend. He became our friend because Jesus took away our sins. Let's thank God for telling us about Himself and for sending Jesus so we can know Him better.

Prayer. Dear God, thank You for giving us the Bible. We know we can trust Your Word. Thank You for giving us Jesus and for keeping His words in the Bible so that we know what He said. We look forward to talking with You in heaven. We pray in the name of Jesus, who took away our sins. Amen.

Every Day

PENTECOST 11: *Ex. 16:2–15; Eph. 4:17–24; John 6:24–35*

Text. When the Israelites saw it, they said to each other, "What is it?" For they did not know what it was. Moses said to them, "It is the bread the LORD has given you to eat." *Ex. 16:15*

Teaching aid. A 12-month calendar.

Gospel nugget. God provides salvation and other blessings to undeserving people.

Who can find today's date on this calendar? (*Allow an older child to locate date.*) That's right. Today is _____ . In one month (*demonstrate*) it will be _____ . This calendar has a whole year of dates, 365 days! How many of these calendars would it take to show 40 years? We would need a stack of 40 calendars like this one. Forty years have more than 14,000 days. Can you imagine having nothing to eat for 14,000 days? That means if you're 7 years old now, you would be hungry until you were 47! Of course, you couldn't live that long without food, and that's what the children of Israel worried about back in the Bible days of Moses.

You may remember the exciting story of how the children of Israel escaped from Egypt. God separated the waters of the Red Sea so Moses could lead the Israelites to safety. Once they were safe, they were also sorry. Having reached the other side of the Red Sea, the Israelites were now in the desert, wondering and wandering. They wondered what they would eat. Some of them complained to Moses, grumbling, "At least we got plenty to eat when we were slaves in Egypt." God heard their complaints and decided to send them food. At first they didn't know what it was, until Moses explained. (*Read text.*) God sent manna to the children of Israel every morning (except Saturdays) for 40 years!

Can you imagine eating the same thing every day from now until you are 45 or 46 or 47 or 48? We might not say "Yuk" about spinach or broccoli or fish if we had to eat the same meal for that many years. You and I might get tired of eating the same thing every day unless, of course, we had absolutely nothing else to eat.

Moses probably reminded the children of Israel that God was keeping them alive by delivering this miracle food each morning. God made it easy for the children of Israel, too. Every day the desert sands were covered with what looked like frost. But it wasn't frost. It was this manna, which the Bible says tasted like crackers made with honey. Every day the children of Israel remained healthy and strong, able to wander in the desert looking for a place to live.

God takes care of us every day, too. Are any of you 7 years old? If you're 7, you were born more than 2,500 days ago. God has taken care of you for all those days, and He will take care of you for the rest of your life.

God doesn't keep us alive with manna anymore. So what does He give us? He blesses us with food and water, the two things necessary for healthy, active bodies. We can even choose from many different-tasting foods and drinks. God gives us doctors and medicines to heal us when we're sick or injured. He gives us family and friends to make us happy and comfortable. We even have books to make us smarter and television to entertain us. God gives us so many things that we could be busy 24 hours a day, 365 days a year, for at least 40 years! We must be careful not to forget the most important blessing He gives us every day.

God fills us with Jesus' love every day. His love forgives us when we act badly. He even loves us when we think that no one else in the whole world loves us. Jesus' love gives us power, power to do good things for others. Jesus' love keeps us alive every day, safe from the devil, who would like to kill us with his evil. God's manna kept the children of Israel alive for 40 years. Jesus' love will keep us alive forever.

Bread and Water

PENTECOST 12: 1 Kings 19:4–8; Eph. 4:30—5:2; John 6:41–51

Text. So he got up and ate and drank. Strengthened by that food, he traveled forty days and forty nights until he reached Horeb, the mountain of God. *1 Kings 19:8*

Teaching aid. A slice of bread and a glass of water on a tray covered with a towel.

Gospel nugget. God restores our strength with the love of Jesus.

Today I'd like to show you the original health foods. (*Unveil tray.*) Bread and water! Did you know that people can live on bread and water alone? Eating only bread and water doesn't sound like much fun, but that's all you need to stay alive.

A prophet named Elijah lived in Bible times. Many people didn't like Elijah because He spoke God's truth, and they didn't want to hear it. Once while he was running away from one of his enemies, Elijah stopped to rest. He told God that he just couldn't go on living this way—always on the run. Poor Elijah was sad and wanted to quit God's work. He just didn't feel successful. So God sent an angel to Elijah with a surprise. Bread and water! That's all Elijah needed to get up and running again. The bread and water filled Elijah's stomach and gave him hope. Bread and water delivered by God's angel helped Elijah remember that God still cared for him. So Elijah kept on working for God.

Jesus once said that He is like bread. He said, "I am the Bread of life." Believing in Jesus is like eating bread—Jesus will keep us alive forever. We can't get to heaven by believing that we are good enough to please God all by ourselves. We can't get to heaven by giving tons of money to the church. We can't get to heaven by asking someone else to pray for us. And we can't get to heaven by obeying laws and rules. The only way to live forever is by believing that Jesus takes away our sins. He is the Bread of eternal life. Knowing that Jesus is the Bread of life makes us like Elijah. He knew God cared for him because God gave him bread.

God also gave Elijah water. Water is the other necessary thing for life. Listen to these words of Jesus: "I tell you the truth, no one can enter the kingdom of God unless he is born of water and the Spirit" (John 3:5). Does that mean that you must be born on a waterbed? No, of course not.

What is water good for besides drinking? Water is good for washing things that are dirty, things like dishes, walls, cars, and even you. How is water used in the church? We use water to baptize people. Baptismal water is what Jesus meant when He said you must be "born of water and the Spirit" to be part of God's kingdom.

God's Holy Spirit works in the water in Baptism. Baptism drowns our sins. It washes us clean for God. Baptism is one of God's ways of keeping us alive forever. Since God gives the gift of Baptism, we know that God cares for each of us, just as He cared for tired old Elijah.

Do you remember what Elijah did after he was refreshed by the bread and water? Listen to today's Bible reading. (*Read text.*) Elijah got get-up-and-go power from the bread and water. That's exactly what Jesus gives us! Now use your energy from Jesus, the Bread and Water of life, to tell others about Jesus. Be kind, helpful, and loving.

Prayer. You are the Bread of life, dear Jesus. Make us strong through Your Word and through Baptism to work for You as we look forward to living forever in heaven. Amen.

Y's Children

PENTECOST 13: Prov. 9:1–6; Eph. 5:15–20; John 6:51–58

Text. Leave your simple ways and you will live; walk in the way of understanding. *Prov. 9:6*

Teaching aid. Sufficient number of capital Y's cut from cardboard for anticipated number of participants; for very large groups, six or eight Y's given to selected volunteers are sufficient.

Gospel nugget. God gives believers faith and wisdom to know salvation through Jesus Christ.

(*Give participants one Y each as they come forward.*) We're going to do a riddle for the people out there. Would all of you stand and face the people? Now hold your Y's up high so everyone can see. Okay, congregation, what do you call this display? These are Y's (wise) children. (*You may wish to remind the congregation that you don't write these talks, you just do them. Reorganize children around you.*)

Has anyone ever called you a "wise guy"? Wise guys are something like "smart alecks." People might call you a wise guy if you play tricks on them. They might call you a smart aleck if you talk back. But today the Bible reading tells us to be truly wise. (*Read text.*) Does being truly wise mean that you should be shaped like this letter? No, of course not. We say you're wise if you understand something the right way. But we'll use our Y's as a shortcut to spell w-i-s-e. Each time I say the word "wise," wave your Y's.

The Bible tells us not be "*wise* guys." As you go to school and become smarter and smarter, you need to be careful not to become "smart alecks." But as you become smarter and smarter, pray that God will make you really *wise*. How can Christian people like you and me become truly *wise*? To find out, let's think about the wisest king who ever served God's people. What was that *wise* king's name? His name was Solomon. How did Solomon become so *wise*? The Bible tells us that God made Solomon *wise*. Did you hear that? Reading, spelling, or math didn't make Solomon *wise*, God did. Besides everything we learn from teachers, we also need to learn from God. Then we can be *wise*, too.

Solomon's father, David, was *wise*, also. In Ps. 19:7 David tells how to get wisdom: "The law of the LORD is perfect, reviving the soul. The statutes of the LORD are trustworthy, making *wise* the simple." David knew that God gives us the Ten Commandments and His other laws to help us be wise. You are truly *wise* when you love God more than you love anyone or anything else. And you are *wise* when you love other people as Jesus did. James, one of Jesus' friends, said it this way: "Who is *wise* and understanding among you? Let him show it by his good life" (James 3:13). Wise people do good deeds for others.

Is it easy to be *wise*? I'm afraid not. We know that God makes us *wise*, but often we don't act that way. Instead of loving God with all of our heart, sometimes we foolishly forget Him. Did you ever stop listening to your Sunday school teacher because something more interesting was going on outside the window? Yep. That's an example of being foolish instead of *wise*.

We don't always do good deeds for others, either. Sometimes we're downright mean. We care more about what we want than what someone else might need. It is indeed hard to be *wise*.

Thank God that Jesus is perfectly *wise*. Because He is perfectly *wise*, Jesus knew what to do about our foolish ways. He forgives us when we don't love God most or we don't love other people. Instead of forgetting about us, He loves us. Keep your Y in a place where it will remind you that God was *wise* in sending Jesus to take away our sins. You are *wise* because you know that Jesus loves you.

Choices _____

PENTECOST 14: Josh. 24:1–2a, 14–18; Eph. 5:21–31; John 6:60–69

Text. But if serving the Lord seems undesirable to you, then choose for yourselves this day whom you will serve, whether the gods your forefathers served beyond the River, or the gods of the Amorites, in whose land you are living. But as for me and my household, we will serve the Lord. *Joshua 24:15*

Teaching aid. One old, short, broken pencil and one new pencil.

Gospel nugget. God chose us to be His children.

I need a volunteer to make a choice. (*Choose one child.*) I'll pick you. I have a present for you, and you get to choose which one you want. Which pencil would you like? (*Allow child to choose.*) Good choice. You picked the best pencil. This beat-up old pencil just wouldn't do much for you.

Have you ever had trouble making up your mind? Perhaps you've had difficulty deciding which flavor ice cream to have or what game to play. Would you have a hard time choosing whether to love God or to love this broken pencil? I hope not.

God has known about you for a long time. He knew you even before your mom and dad knew you. God chose you to be His child back when He was creating the world. He even knew what your name would be.

Now I hope I don't hurt your feelings, but God didn't pick you because you behave so well or because you're so pretty or handsome. God didn't choose you because you have so much faith or because you go to church and Sunday school. God chose you to be His child because He loves you. Look around you. God chose all of us for only one reason—He loves us.

Wouldn't it be terrible if God didn't want us! How frightened we would be if we couldn't count on God to protect us. How sad we would be if Grandma or Grandpa died, and we didn't know they were living in heaven. How lonely we would feel if Jesus didn't love us every moment. How unhappy we would be if we didn't know that God forgives us. But God did choose us. He wants us.

What is surprising and sad is that lots of people don't want God. Long ago Joshua knew that. Listen to what he said. (*Read text.*) People chose a different god. I'll describe him. He wants you very much. He is very powerful. He gets you into all kinds of trouble, and he laughs when you are hurt or angry. It's very easy to do what he wants, but it's very hard to ever be happy. Whom did they choose? They chose the devil.

Joshua said he and his family would choose God instead. Why? Because God wants you very much. He made you His child long before you were born, but He doesn't force you to remain His child. He is very powerful, even more powerful than the devil. He forgives you when you get into trouble because He sent His Son to take away your sins. Sometimes it's hard to do what He wants, but He loves you even when you fail. Choice number 2 is God, the God who already chose you.

Which do you choose, God or the devil? Do you want to hear some great news? God knows we have trouble making the right choice, so He helps us choose Him. Not just one time. He helps us choose Him even after we've chosen the devil. Because the devil is like this broken old pencil. (*Display pencil.*) He can't help you in any way. He is useless.

God always knows what is best for us. He sent Jesus to die for our sins, and He helps us to live in ways that please Him. Because God chose us, we can choose Him. Let's have three cheers for our good God. Ready? (*Lead children in cheers.*)

Good God! Good God! Good God!

Always Near

PENTECOST 15: Deut. 4:1–2, 6–8; Eph. 6:10–20; Mark 7:1–8, 14–15, 21–23

Text. What other nation is so great as to have their gods near them the way the Lord our God is near us whenever we pray to him? *Deut. 4:7*

Teaching aid. Folding or other easy-to-carry chair.

Gospel nugget. God answers our prayers for Jesus' sake.

(*Place chair away from group where it will not distract participants.*) Let's begin by saying the Lord's Prayer together. (*Pray together.*)

What a wonderful prayer! Everything we need to pray for is already in the Lord's Prayer. We said, "Give us this day our daily bread." Will you eat today? "Daily" and "bread" are two short words with very big meanings. When we ask God to give us our "daily bread" we really mean that we need food, clothing, home, and everything else for safe and healthy lives. We depend on God to grow vegetables, trees, and other plants. God provides animals for food, too.

We also ask God to forgive us in the Lord's Prayer. We know He sent Jesus to take away our sins, so when we ask God to forgive us, we can be sure that He does. Of course, God expects us to forgive other people as much as He forgives us. That's a lot, isn't it?

We also ask God to protect us from the devil and to keep us from doing bad things. How does God protect us from the devil? He sends angels to protect us. Best of all, He sent Jesus to take away the devil's power. The devil wants to make us his children. But Jesus won't let him. God helps us avoid bad behavior by teaching us right from wrong. Sometimes we do wrong anyway. Then Jesus forgives us.

Think back to the first words of the Lord's Prayer. (*Softly say, "Our Father in heaven"*) Where is God? Yes, we pray to God in heaven. But where is heaven? Heaven seems so far away. Maybe we should shout our prayers so God can hear us! But we don't really need to yell because God is someplace else, too. (*Get chair and place it in middle of group. Sit or stand next to empty chair.*) God is as close to us as this chair.

What! How can God be way off in heaven and also as close as this chair? That's the great thing about God! He is everywhere at once. He is with us right here. Listen to today's Bible reading. (*Read text.*) He's also at your house (*point to other children*) and your house and your house. Then He's also with other children thousands of miles away in England and China and Africa. God is always close to us.

What good comes from having God so near? God is always close enough to know what we need. Even though we can't see Him, He is as close as this chair. We can sit at His feet and chat with Him. He wants to know how you are feeling today. When you have a stomachache or your head hurts, God listens carefully to you and does what is best. When you are happy, God probably smiles. Maybe He says something like, "That's right, be happy. I sent Jesus to save you, and I don't want you to worry about a thing." And what do you think would happen if you had to tell God, "I haven't been as good as you want me to be"? Would you expect God to holler at you? Would you expect Him to say, "Get out of my sight. You're not good enough"? No. God would say, "I forgive you, because Jesus died for you."

Next time you pray, look around the room. God is as close to you as the nearest chair or bed or table.

Let's talk to God now.

Prayer. Dear God, thank You for being right here with us for Jesus' sake. Amen.

Back to Normal

PENTECOST 16: Is. 35:4–7a; James 1:17–22 (23–25), 26–27; Mark 7:31–37

Text. Say to those with fearful hearts, "Be strong, do not fear; your God will come, He will come with vengeance; with divine retribution He will come to save you." Then will the eyes of the blind be opened and the ears of the deaf unstopped. Then will the lame leap like a deer, and the mute tongue shout for joy. Water will gush forth in the wilderness and streams in the desert. The burning sand will become a pool, the thirsty ground bubbling springs. *Is. 35:4–7a*

Teaching aid. Dry washcloth and wet washcloth.

Gospel nugget. When Jesus returns, He will give us perfect lives in heaven, where we will glorify Him.

We will use two washcloths to get us started today. (*Select a child.*) How does this washcloth feel? Now how does this one feel? One cloth is wet, and the other is dry. Wet and dry are opposites. What is the opposite of bad? (*Encourage responses.*) What is the opposite of sick? And what is the opposite of dead? You know your opposites very well.

Please listen for opposites in these Bible verses. (*Read text emphasizing the opposites.*) What does God say will happen to blind eyes? Yes, they will be opened so they can see again. Deaf people can't hear. What will happen to their ears? That's right. The Bible says their ears will be unstopped so they can hear again.

Next we heard about lame people. How does a lame person walk? (*Allow someone to demonstrate.*) Can you imagine a lame person running like a deer? That would be a wonderful opposite. God mentions a mute tongue. Persons with mute tongues can't talk or sing. But the Bible says they will be the opposite. What will happen to them? Yes, they'll be able to shout with delight.

What do you know about deserts? Little rain falls in the desert, so it's very dry. It would be difficult to live in the desert. The Bible said deserts will become the opposite of dry, full of rivers and water where there once was only dry desert!

When will all these opposites happen? Jesus made many of these opposites happen already. While He was on earth, Jesus healed people who had different sicknesses. The Bible tells us that He made some blind people see and that He made deaf people hear. Jesus once changed a storm into calm and made wine from ordinary water. He even made several dead people alive again.

Jesus wasn't a magician. He was God's own Son. He had all of God's power. Jesus never used His great powers to hurt people. He only helped them.

Do you think Jesus will ever make so many opposites again? He will! When Jesus comes to take us to heaven, He will change everything. Jesus will change everything back to the way that's normal for God. Only the most perfect things are normal for God. Only the best things are normal for God. Way back when God started the world and created everything, He made all things perfect. When Jesus comes to take us to heaven, everything will be perfect again. He'll even make dead people alive so they can enjoy heaven with Him forever.

Let's make up a prayer thanking Jesus for the opposites He'll make in heaven. I'll start each part of the prayer and you can finish it with an opposite.

We praise you, Jesus, because You will make sad people *(pause for response)* _____ .

We praise You, Jesus, because You will make bad people

_____ .

We praise You, Jesus, because You will make dead people

_____ .

(Add others as appropriate.)

Thank You, Jesus, for all your love. Amen.

He Did It

PENTECOST 17: Is. 50:4–10; James 2:1–5, 8–10, 14–18; Mark 8:27–35

Text. He who vindicates me is near. Who then will bring charges against me? Let us face each other! Who is my accuser? Let him confront me! *Is. 50:8*

Teaching aid. A large arrow cut from cardboard. Also locate in the worship area a statue, stained-glass window, etc., of Jesus before beginning the message.

Gospel nugget. Jesus will defend us against the devil's accusations.

Listen to this story about Debbie and Donald. They were sister and brother who got along well together most of the time. One day while they were playing ball in the yard, Debbie accidentally kicked the ball into Mr. Danner's flower bed. The ball broke the buds off a few petunias and geraniums. Mr. Danner didn't say a word. He just looked at Debbie and Donald. It was hard to tell whether he was angry or sad. Suddenly, Donald pointed a finger (*demonstrate with arrow*) at Debbie and said, "She did it, Mr. Danner. She did it." Debbie felt bad about breaking Mr. Danner's flowers, and she felt hurt because Donald told on her.

Has anyone told on you (*point with arrow*) when you did something wrong? It seems like someone is always ready to let others know what we're doing.

"He did it. He did it." "She did it. She did it." Those are the words of tattletales who like to get others into trouble. If someone does something really wrong, like touching us where we don't want to be touched or trying to get us to ride in a strange car, then it's perfectly okay to tell. But often, tattletales tell about little, unimportant things to get others into trouble, don't they?

Someone already knows everything that we've ever done wrong. He's just itching to tell on us. He wants us to get into trouble with God! Can you guess whom I'm talking about? It's the devil. He's so sneaky and mean!

The devil just loves to see us do wrong. In fact, he helps us get into trouble. The devil tempts everyone. The devil is the one who told Eve and Adam that they didn't need to obey God.

The devil even tempted Jesus. He picked a good time to do it, too. He waited until Jesus was lonely, hungry, and tired. Then he tried to get Jesus to disobey God the Father. But Jesus wouldn't give in. Jesus is the only one who never gave in to the devil. He did what we can't do.

Every time the devil sees us doing something bad, he runs off to God— yes, to God—and tells on us. The devil probably thinks that God will hate us. When you think of the devil, think of a big arrow like this one. The devil points at you, saying, "She did it, God. She slapped her sister when Mom wasn't looking." The devil points at you and says, "He did it, God. Another sin! He wouldn't put on his pajamas when Dad said it was time for bed. Isn't he terrible?"

When the devil sneers at us and says, "He did it. She did it," remember what today's Bible reading promises. (*Read text.*) God is near when Satan points his finger at us, and He says, "I don't see any sinners here." He asks one very important question. "Who took your sins away and saved you?"

Then we can answer God by saying (*point at Jesus figure*), "He did it. He did it."

Prayer. Dear God, forgive us for Jesus' sake. He suffered and died for us. He beat the devil because we're too weak to do it ourselves. Thank You for sending Jesus to do it for us. Amen.

From Beginning to End

PENTECOST 18: Jer. 11:18–20; James 3:16–4:6; Mark 9:30–37

Text. Because the LORD revealed their plot to me, I knew it, for at that time he showed me what they were doing. *Jer. 11:18*

Teaching aid. A Bible marked to find the first verse (Gen. 1:1) and the last verse (Rev. 22:21) as well as Jeremiah and Lamentations

Gospel nugget. Although we are subject to many temptations and attacks, God strengthens our faith with His plan of salvation.

(*Hold up Bible.*) Could you read this big Bible from the beginning to the end? Of course you probably can't do it now, but someday you'll be able to read the whole book. Would you like me to read it to you from beginning to end? Probably not right now. It would take many days to read the whole Bible. Maybe you would like to hear the beginning and the end of God's Book. Since most stories begin at the front of the book, I'll read the very first verse. (*Read Gen. 1:1.*) Wow! That really is the beginning, isn't it? God created the heaven and the earth.

We will skip all these pages in the middle and go to the end of God's Book. (*Read Rev. 22:21.*) The Bible ends with the word *Amen.* Many stories end with the words *The End,* but the Bible ends with "Amen." We end our prayers by saying "Amen," too. Amen means that we believe every word of God is true. This great big book (*indicate Bible*) is God's true story about how much He loves us.

All stories have characters. Sometimes the characters are people, and sometimes they are animals. Some characters are good, and some are bad. God's book tells about many people. Some believed in God, and some hated Him. Do you know the names of any people in the Bible who loved God? (*Invite responses.*)

Jeremiah was one man who believed in God. Look here. (*Open Bible to Jeremiah*). This is how his name is spelled. (*Hold pages of Jeremiah and Lamentations between your fingers.*) This part of the Bible tells about how God used Jeremiah to speak to His people, but they didn't want to hear about God's plan for their lives. They wanted to do whatever pleased them instead of what pleased God. They didn't want to worship the true God. People wanted to worship idols or false gods. They invented these make-believe gods, and when Jeremiah told the people they were wrong, the people became angry. They hated Jeremiah, just as they hated God, and they tried to hurt Jeremiah. But God helped Jeremiah. Today's Bible reading tells how God helped him. (*Read text.*)

The Bible tells many true stories like the one about Jeremiah. The Bible is God's Book about how He made the whole world and everything else. It's God's story about how He sent Jesus to save us from our enemy the devil, and how He takes care of all His people.

You're in God's story, too. You might or might not find a name like yours in this book (*indicate Bible*), but God talks about you. He says that He sent Jesus to take away your sins. He says He gave you the Holy Spirit so you could worship Him and live His way. People might not always like you if you live God's way, but God tells you, through stories like Jeremiah, that God's enemies can never take you away from Him. What great news! We're safe with God. We're saved by Jesus.

We'll end today's message with the words at the end of the Bible. (*Read Rev. 22:21 directly from Bible.*)

Help!

PENTECOST 19: *Num. 11:4–6, 10–16, 24–29; James 4:7–12 (13–5:6); Mark 9:38–50*

Text. I wish that all the LORD's people were prophets and that the LORD would put his Spirit on them!" *Num. 11:29*

Teaching aid. An unopened can of food.

Gospel nugget. God sends helpers to proclaim the Gospel and to help His people.

I have a million-dollar reward for any of you who can open this can right now. (*Place can in front of children.*) Would anyone like to try? Could you open it if two or three of you tried to do it together? I guess you would still need help. What would you need to open this can? Only a can opener could help you open the can.

With what other things do you need help? (*Encourage responses. Share something with which you need assistance.*) We all need help at times.

Even Moses needed help. As great a worker for God as Moses was, he still couldn't work alone. When God first asked Moses to work for Him, Moses had all kinds of excuses. He thought God's work was too hard. So God gave helpers to Moses. Some of them could do things that Moses couldn't do well at all. One helper was Aaron, Moses' brother. God used Aaron to speak to God's people because Moses wasn't a very good talker. Moses often called to God for help, and God always helped Moses do the job. Once, when some of Moses' friends complained that others were doing the work he should have been doing, Moses said, "I wish that all the LORD's people were prophets and that the LORD would put His Spirit on them!" (Num. 11:29). Moses was glad for all the help he could get.

Sometimes we enjoy doing things ourselves. The first time you tie your shoes by yourself makes you feel really good. But you can't learn to tie shoes by yourself. You need someone to help you, to teach you how. When you learn to read, it feels so good to say the words as you read a story. But sometimes you get stuck on new words. Then it feels good to get some help so that you know the word the next time you see it. If you learned how to swim, you wouldn't need anyone to keep you floating. But if you became sick or injured while swimming, you would want someone to rescue you. No matter how good we get, we always need help with something.

Who helps you know more about Jesus? (*Encourage responses.*) The Holy Spirit helps parents, pastors, teachers, and me tell you about Jesus. Can you tell others how much Jesus loves them? You can tell others who don't already know about Jesus. But even those who already know that Jesus loves them enjoy hearing the good news again.

You can share Jesus' love, too. People who know Jesus' love are kind, helpful, and forgiving. Can you be kind and helpful to someone this week? Who needs your help? (*Allow time for responses.*) Jesus taught us how to live. He said, "Follow my example."

Who might need forgiveness this week? All of us need forgiveness, and we need it often. Getting forgiveness by ourselves is like trying to open this can without help. It's impossible. But you know where to find that kind of help. Jesus does the job for you. His help is like the help a lifeguard gives a drowning swimmer. Without it we would end up far away from God. When we sinners cry, "Help! Help!" Jesus helps us by taking away our sins.

Prayer. Help us! Help us, Lord Jesus. We need You every day. And send us Your Holy Spirit to help us help others. Amen.

Partners

PENTECOST 20: Gen. 2:18–24; Heb. 2:9–11 (12–18); Mark 10:2–16

Text. The LORD God said, "It is not good for the man to be alone. I will make a helper suitable for him." *Gen. 2:18*

Teaching aid. A supply of regular-size paper clips and several large paper clips.

Gospel nugget. God's forgiveness enables earthly families to live in His love as partners.

Did you ever feel lonely? People feel lonely when there is no one else around with whom to talk, play, or work.

When God created Adam, he was the only person in the whole world. God told Adam to enjoy himself, and God gave Adam a perfect garden for a home. Every kind of animal lived in the garden. Adam's job was to name them. What fun it must have been to name that animal with really long legs, a short tail, and a very, very, very, very long neck! What did Adam name that animal? We still like giraffes today. As much fun as it was to name all the animals, Adam didn't find even one that could really keep him company. God knew that Adam needed someone like himself for a partner. (*Quote text.*) So God created Eve to be Adam's partner. Adam and Eve were the first husband and wife. They were partners in the pleasant work God gave them in their garden home. Adam and Eve were happy, and they loved each other very much. Later they would become the first Mom and Dad.

God, Adam, and Eve were like these paper clips. (*Use a large clip to represent God. Hook two small—regular size—paper clips to the first to form a chain.*) They were attached to each other.

God, Adam, and Eve were a family. God blesses us with families today, too.

All Christian families start with God (*indicate first/large clip*). Why is it good to have God in your family? God helps families to love and forgive each other. God helps families to be partners. God helps when it is hard to get along, and He shows us how to be kind and to work together. God keeps families together.

Who is in your family? (*Choose a child known to have a two-parent family to answer.*) Mom, Dad, and you. (*String together three or more regular paper clips.*) Who else is in your family? Yes, let's be sure to say that God is part of your family. (*Add large clip to chain—attach each end to the large clip to make a circular chain.*)

Some families have one parent at home with the kids. So for this kind of family we have God at the beginning (*large clip*) and Mom or Dad and the kids. (*Add two or more clips to the large one to form a circle.*) Sometimes the Mom of one family marries the Dad of another family and together they become one new family. (*Attach two strings of clips*). Who belongs with this family, too? Why God, of course! (*Attach both ends to large clip.*)

God belongs with every kind of family. Even if you were all alone without a mom or dad or brother or sister, you would still be part of God's family. God made you and your family partners with Jesus. God was Jesus' Father, and God calls us His children, too. That makes Jesus our brother. Wow! What a brother! Brother Jesus took all the punishment we should get for not living the way God the Father wants us to live. He took away our sins so we could live together as one big happy family with God our heavenly Father.

Let's thank God for our families.

Prayer. Dear God, thank You for my family and thank You for being part of it. Help us live together like partners with our brother Jesus. Amen.

God Is with You

PENTECOST 21: Amos 5:6–7, 10–15; Heb. 3:1–6; Mark 10:17–27, (28–30)

Text. Seek good, not evil, that you may live. Then the LORD God Almighty will be with you, just as you say he is. *Amos 5:14*

Teaching aid. Two boxes with covers—one marked *Good* and the other *Evil*. Place a Bible inside the "good" box.

Gospel nugget. Jesus is with us to help us choose good.

Look at the two boxes in front of you. Let's have a volunteer read the words on top of each box. (*Select a volunteer*). Which box would you choose to open, good or evil? I would select good also. Let's see what's inside the good box. (*Remove top.*) Ah, a Bible. Should we also see what's inside the evil box? I'll peek (*peek just under top*). Hmm. I don't see a thing. What can you see? (*Remove top and show children.*) Nothing. Nothing in the box marked evil. Which would you rather have, God's word (*hold up Bible*) or nothing at all. (*Indicate empty box.*)

Life without God is evil. Don't you think everyone would want to have God in their lives? But even people who want God to live with them sometimes choose evil instead of good. I know I do that. That's the reason Amos, one of God's prophets, said (*read text*). We need that reminder.

Do you think we would act differently if we saw Jesus sitting here with us. How might we act? (*Anticipate moralistic answers.*) We might want Him to think that we're always very good. But Jesus knows we're not always good. He doesn't love us because we're good. He loves us because He is good, and because we need His love.

Maybe we would act happier if we saw Jesus sitting here. We might run up and hug and kiss Him. We would probably listen carefully as Jesus spoke. We would want to hear those wonderful words over and over: *I love you. You'll always belong to Me.* And when we prayed, instead of closing our eyes, we could look right into Jesus' eyes, sure that He would answer us. We would leave church ready to do whatever He told us, and we could hardly wait until next Sunday to be with Him again.

Well, Jesus is here, even though we can't see Him. He will go home with us, too. And when we go outside, Jesus will be right there. We can be as happy as if we could see Jesus.

Do you know why Jesus is with us? Because we don't choose good (*indicate box*) instead of evil (*indicate other box*). Jesus helps us. For example, suppose Mom's grocery sack ripped open, and cans and bottles and boxes flew all over the kitchen floor. What would you do? You might ignore Mom's problem or make fun of her. But, if you remembered that Jesus, your friend who helps you, was there, you would probably want to help Mom. Jesus would help you choose good.

Let's see if you can choose good again. Imagine that your friend just got a new red bicycle. He's racing it around and showing off in front of you. Then he yells, "Hey, look at me. I've got the greatest bike in the world. Your bike looks ugly." Before he can say any other mean things, he runs into a tree and falls to the ground, hurt and bleeding and crying. His bike is twisted and bent. Knowing that Jesus lives with you, and remembering what Jesus did for people who were mean to Him, what would you do? You would try to help your friend get up, or you could call for help. Or you could say, "I'm sorry you and your bike got so messed up." Jesus is with us to help us say hard things like that when people make us angry or sad. While Jesus was dying on the cross, He asked God to forgive His enemies. He prayed for all of us, and then He died to save us.

Prayer. Dear Jesus, thank You for being with us always. Make us more like You. Help us to choose good. We know how empty life would be without You. Thank You for telling us about Yourself in the Bible. Amen.

Lots and Lots

PENTECOST 22: Is. 53:10–12; Heb. 4:9–16; Mark 10:35–45

Text. After the suffering of His soul, He will see the light of life and be satisfied; by His knowledge My righteous Servant will justify many, and He will bear their iniquities. *Is. 53:11*

Teaching aid. A hymnal and a transparent container or bag filled with anything such as macaroni, rice, beans, etc.; a second *larger* container with the same contents.

Gospel nugget. Through His death and resurrection, Jesus justified us so we are righteous before God.

Guess how many pieces of macaroni are in this bag? (*Accept guesses.*) One thing is certain, many pieces of macaroni, perhaps too many to count, are in this bag. Yet it's easy to pick up this bag. It is light. But what if each piece of macaroni were as heavy as this book? (*Pass around hymnal.*) Would you be able to carry a bag holding 100 hymnals? It would be too heavy! What if each of the macaroni weighed as much as you do? A bag of them would be far too heavy for almost anyone to carry.

Today we want to think about how Jesus carried the sins of every person who ever lived. Look around you. Every person here does wrong things each day. I don't know how much each sin weighs, but God asked Jesus to carry all of them to the cross and to die to take them away from you and me. Our sins will never be counted against us.

Why did Jesus do that? Yes, He loves us so much. His love is bigger than our sins. If this first bag is like our sins, then this second bag is like Jesus' love and forgiveness. (*Place the larger container under the lesser bag.*) See, Jesus' love easily holds up the weight of our sins.

Sins hurt us. It hurts other people, too. If you talk back to Mom at home, she will feel hurt and sad, and she might not let you watch TV for awhile to punish you.

If you run out into a street while playing even though Dad warned you not to, you can get hurt. A car or truck might run over you. That's what happens sometimes when you disobey.

All of us suffer just because sin is in the world. Have you ever been sick? What did you have? (*Encourage responses.*) God never wants anyone to be sick. Sicknesses began after Adam and Eve and everyone else became sinners.

So far my talk hasn't been about happy things. Maybe we don't like to hear about how sins ruin our fun, or how Jesus took each of our sins and suffered for them. But it would be a lot scarier if we had to live with the devil in hell because we are sinners.

Thank God for Jesus. He carried all our sins away, even though they were very heavy. Now He is happy He did it. Isaiah the prophet tells us why. (*Read text.*) Since Jesus carried our sins away, God doesn't see our sins. Instead, because we trust Jesus, God sees us without our sin.

Someday, when Jesus takes us to heaven, we'll get to see Jesus and thank Him for carrying away our sins. We'll see lots and lots of other people whose sins Jesus also took away. But let's not wait till then to thank Him. Will you pray with me?

Prayer. Dear Savior, we know our sins caused You much pain and suffering. Thank You for carrying them away so God can't see them. We look forward to the day when we see You. Amen.

Lost and Found

PENTECOST 23: Jer. 31:7–9; Heb. 5:1–10; Mark 10:46–52

Text. They will come with weeping; they will pray as I bring them back. I will lead them beside streams of water on a level path where they will not stumble, because I am Israel's father, and Ephraim is my firstborn son. *Jer. 31:9*

Teaching aid. A can of soup (or any foodstuff).

Gospel nugget. The Savior leads the lost to salvation.

Have you ever been lost in a store or some other crowded place? This can of soup reminds me of a boy named Jason who got lost in the World's Largest Grocery Store.

Jason was shopping with his father at the World's Largest Grocery Store. Now Jason was 6-going-on-7, and he thought he was too old to be holding Dad's hand. Jason walked right next to his father through the sausage and cheese department. He stayed next to his dad through housewares and soaps. The fruit and vegetable department was just ahead. Jason asked, "Can we stop to look at the lettuce and the apples and the onions?" (Jason just loved the smells and colors and shapes of different fruits and vegetables displayed side by side.)

Jason's dad answered, "Not today. I have some work at home, and we need to hurry. . . . Let's see, Mom wanted a can of tomato soup."

Jason was disappointed, but he kept on walking next to his dad until he just had to stop and look at the celery, squash, and avocados. He stopped, all right, but Jason's father kept walking. Jason picked up a huge garlic bulb to get a closer look. He was about to say, "Hey Dad, can we buy one of these?" when he noticed that Dad wasn't there. He felt sick inside, and he was very frightened. He ran from aisle to aisle searching for Dad. He bumped into grocery carts and tripped over shoppers' feet. Jason even ran to the soup department, but Dad wasn't there. Jason started to cry. Suddenly, a warm, strong hand clasped his shoulder. Jason froze. He looked up. It was Dad. What a relief! You see, while Jason was hunting for his father, his father had gone looking for him. Today's Bible reading says God is like Jason's dad. Listen. (*Read text.*)

Lost. That's what we are without Jesus. People who are lost are usually afraid. They don't know where they are, and they don't know where to go. All they can do is wait for someone to help them. God sent Jesus to find lost people and to bring them to Him.

What kind of lost people does Jesus find? Some lost people have never heard about Jesus. They may not even know that they are lost! They have no idea that a Savior loves them and wants them. Jesus finds these people. Sometimes he uses missionaries, special pastors, to look for them. Often Jesus uses ordinary people like you and me to tell others about Jesus.

Jesus also looks for another kind of lost people. These lost people once walked with Jesus and went where Jesus wanted them to go, but they became interested in things that Jesus didn't want them to do. Maybe they thought they didn't need to listen to their parents, so they did only what they wanted. Perhaps they thought that using bad language was more fun, more grown-up, than talking as God desires. Maybe they were so angry that they forgot about forgiveness, and instead hurt someone. There are lots of ways to be lost in sin.

Jesus finds those lost people, too. He comes looking for us even when we don't want Him to find us. He forgives us and wants us back with Him. Let's always try to stay close to Jesus, and let's remember that God keeps looking for us.

Prayer. Lord Jesus, You found us and made us Your children. Send Your Holy Spirit to keep us close to You. Amen.

Remember

PENTECOST 24: Deut. 6:1–9; Heb. 7:23–28; Mark 12:28–34 (35–37)

Text. Hear, O Israel, and be careful to obey so that it may go well with you and that you may increase greatly in a land flowing with milk and honey, just as the LORD, the God of your fathers, promised you. . . . These commandments that I give you today are to be upon your hearts. . . . Tie them as symbols on your hands and bind them on your foreheads. Deut. 6:3, 6, 8

Teaching aid. A piece of string or yarn tied around your index finger. Optional: Supply of short pieces of yarn to tie around participants' fingers.

Gospel nugget. God helps us remember His love is for us and others.

Do you have any tricks to help you remember things that you shouldn't forget? Some people write down what they should remember. If Grandma's birthday is on Dec. 6, Mom might write "Grandma's Birthday" on the calendar. People shopping in a grocery store make a list so they don't forget to buy what they really need.

Look at my finger. An old saying goes, If you want to remember something, tie a string around your finger. I tied this string on my finger so I would remember that Jesus loves me. (*Optional: If you would like a string to help you remember that Jesus loves you, too, I'll be glad to tie one around your finger while I'm talking.*)

God's people sometimes have a bad habit of forgetting that Jesus loves them. Back in Bible days, God's people were called the children of Israel. Although God rescued the children of Israel from many troubles, they often forgot Him. Whenever they forgot about God's love, they became very unhappy. They would grumble and argue and get into fights. Sometimes they even made make-believe gods and prayed to them! But God never forgot the children of Israel. He was always ready to forgive them and to bless their lives with love again. God cared for the children of Israel so much that He also told them how they could remember Him. (*Read text.*) That's kind of like tying a string around your finger, isn't it? God gave His children—the children of Israel—the Commandments to help them remember Him.

By the time Jesus was born, the children of Israel had so many rules for remembering God that they would have had to wrap their whole bodies in string.

So, when baby Jesus grew into a man, He said to remember one rule: Love. Love God. Love others. Love God and others just as Jesus loves you.

This string around my finger reminds me that Jesus loves me. It also reminds me to love God and all the people in the whole world. God sent Jesus for you and me and everyone else. After He suffered for our sins and died on the cross, He rose from the dead. Now He says to us, "I love you all so much that you won't stay dead either. You'll live with Me in heaven."

Today, God's people are called Christians. God gives Christians Bible stories so they can remember how much He loves them. God listens to Jesus and the Holy Spirit when They talk about us. Jesus says to God, "See all those sinners down there? Sometimes they forget about You and Me, but I died for them. They're really Your children."

The Holy Spirit says to God, "I'll go and stay in their hearts because they are so special to You. I'll help them love You. I'll help them love Your other people, too."

Prayer. Dear God, thank You for loving each of us. Help us always to love You. For Jesus' sake we pray. Amen.

Filled Up

PENTECOST 25: 1 Kings 17:8–16; Heb. 9:24–28; Mark 12:41–44

Text. For this is what the LORD, the God of Israel, says: "The jar of flour will not be used up and the jug of oil will not run dry until the day the LORD gives rain on the land." She went away and did as Elijah had told her. So there was food every day for Elijah and for the woman and her family. *1 Kings 17:14–15*

Teaching aid. One cracker.

Gospel nugget. The Savior's love is in constant supply.

(Engage children in a discussion of the following questions.) How would you feel if this one cracker was all you had to eat? What would happen if this cracker was the last thing you could ever eat? Would you feel much like sharing the cracker if it was your last piece of food?

Today's Bible story from the Old Testament tells about a mother and her son. They had only one meal left before they would run out of food. Farmers in their neighborhood couldn't grow food to sell to this woman because there had been no rain to water the seeds and plants.

As she was preparing the last meal for herself and her son, a stranger came to town and asked her to give him some food. The stranger's name was Elijah. God told Elijah to ask this woman for food, though He knew that the woman had only enough for one last meal before she and her son would die of hunger.

Elijah promised the woman that she would always have enough food. God would supply what she needed. The woman believed Elijah and shared her food with him. And God did supply her with food. Even though she baked bread with her last few cups of flour and oil, God always kept the flour and oil jars full. He kept the woman, her son, and Elijah from starving.

The story of Elijah and the starving woman had a happy ending, didn't it? God did a miracle to keep them alive. God did another miracle to keep us living, too. We need God's love to live happily every day. We also need His love so that we can live forever with Jesus.

God's supply of love is like the air around us. You can't see air because it's invisible, but you know it's there anyway, because air is everywhere. Swish your hand back and forth and you can feel the air even though you can't see it. Take a deep breath (*demonstrate*). You are breathing invisible air to keep you alive. Did we use up all the air when we breathed together? No, we're still breathing. We have enough air for all of us.

God's love works the same way. We can never use it up. Each time God forgives us for doing something wrong, He is loving us. But no matter how often we use God's forgiveness, we can never use it up. He fills us with love every time we need it.

God loves us with the Bible, too. His words are in the Bible. He tells us over and over how much He loves us. And no matter how often we hear about His love, it always sounds good. God's Word makes us happy.

God loves us by always being near. He says that He will always take care of us. When we're in danger, He's there to help. When we're sleeping, He watches over us. Thousands of miles away, God is doing the same for His other children in Australia or New Guinea or India. God never runs out of care even though He cares for all people.

The best thing about God's endless supply of love is that it's free to us. It doesn't cost us even a penny. Like the supply of flour in the poor woman's kitchen, we always have enough of God's love.

Prayer. Thank You, dear God, for Your endless supply of love. Help us share Your love with everyone we meet. We pray in Jesus' name. Amen.

Shining Christians

Third Last Sunday in the Church Year:
Dan. 12:1–3; Heb. 12:26–29 or Heb. 10:11–18; Mark 13:1–13

Text. At that time Michael, the great prince who protects your people, will arise. There will be a time of distress such as has not happened from the beginning of nations until then. But at that time your people—everyone whose name is found written in the book—will be delivered. . . . Those who are wise will shine like the brightness of the heavens, and those who lead many to righteousness, like the stars for ever and ever. *Dan. 12:1, 3*

Teaching aid. A tablet of paper (several if you anticipate many participants) and one or more pencils.

Gospel nugget. The Lord will take all the righteous to eternal life on the last day.

Let's make a list of everyone's first name. If you can write your first name, please put it on this tablet. I'll help those who haven't yet learned to write their names. (*Assist younger children, printing their names for them to see. When all names are recorded, read them aloud as if you were taking attendance.*)

The Bible talks about God having a book in which our names are written. Let's listen to the book of Daniel. (*Read text.*) God knows your name! He knows (*read children's names again*).

The Bible book of Daniel tells us about what will happen when Jesus comes to take His people to their home in heaven. The day Jesus returns is called Judgment Day. This will be a frightening day for those who don't believe that Jesus saved them from their sins. But for you and me who believe Jesus saved us, Judgment Day will be the biggest celebration ever. Let me tell you more about Judgment Day.

Surprise! Surprise! When Jesus comes for us, it will be a surprise. The Bible doesn't tell us when Jesus will return, but God promises to take us home to heaven, so we can be certain that Jesus is coming again. Sometime. Someday.

Would you like to know more about Judgment Day? Not only will it be a big surprise, but it will be a big party. A huge crowd will gather on Judgment Day. In fact, all the people who ever lived will be together, more people than any of us has ever seen. Then we'll see God and His book—the one with our names in it. Can you imagine God opening that gigantic book and reading the names of all the people who have believed that Jesus took away their sins? The list will be long. We'll hear (*read children's names again*). Then all of us will gather around Jesus in our new heavenly home.

You wrote your names on my paper today. Do you know who wrote your names in God's book? The Holy Spirit put your names there when He made you a Christian. (Do you remember that the Holy Spirit is another name for God?) We can thank the Holy Spirit, and, of course, Jesus, too. If it wasn't for Jesus, our names couldn't be in God's book. Only the names of holy people appear in God's book. We must be perfect in order to be holy. That's where Jesus comes in. He takes away our sins so we look holy to God.

Soon we'll be thinking about Christmas again. Jesus surprised everyone by coming as a baby. The next time He comes we'll see Him as our King. He will shine like the brightest star. We'll shine brightly, too, because Jesus made us holy.

Let's thank God in prayer.

Prayer. Dear Father, thank You for making us wise. We believe Jesus took away our sins, and we praise the Holy Spirit for writing our names in Your book. We look forward to meeting You face to face so we can say, "I love You God." In Jesus' holy name we pray. Amen.

God's Court

Second Last Sunday in the Church Year: Dan. 7:9–10; Heb. 12:1–2 or Heb. 13:20–21; Mark 13:24–31

Text. As I looked, thrones were set in place, and the Ancient of Days took his seat. His clothing was as white as snow; the hair of his head was white like wool. His throne was flaming with fire, and its wheels were all ablaze. A river of fire was flowing, coming out from before him. Thousands upon thousands attended him; ten thousand times ten thousand stood before him. The court was seated, and the books were opened. . . . there . . . was one like a son of man, coming with the clouds of heaven. . . . all peoples, nations and men of every language worshiped Him. . . . His kingdom is one that will never be destroyed. *Dan. 7:9–10, 13, 14*

Teaching aid. A gavel. (If no gavel is available, a hammer may be an acceptable substitute if you explain the similarity.)

Gospel nugget. When God holds court on Judgment Day, Jesus will successfully plead the case of Christians.

When a judge enters the courtroom, there is a brief ceremony to honor the judge. Everybody stands when the judge enters to show that he is in charge of the court. The judge, usually dressed in a black robe, sits down and bangs a gavel (*hammer*) like this one as a sign that he is ready to decide if a person is guilty of some crime like driving too fast or stealing money.

Our Bible story for today tells about a heavenly court. Listen while I read from Daniel 7. (*Read adapted text above.*)

The Judge's name is the "Ancient of Days." That's just another way of saying that God Himself is the Judge. He's dressed in bright white clothing. His courtroom is the whole world. Too many people to count attend the court session. You see, it's the court at the end of the world, Judgment Day.

Can you imagine God sitting on a fiery throne? He won't get burned because He is God. Even fire can't hurt Him. Daniel mentions a river of fire, too. Have you ever seen a river made of fire? Sounds scary to me. But we won't be afraid of God on Judgment Day. You see, we have someone to tell God that we belong to Him. Who do you think will do that for us?

Jesus will tell God that we belong in heaven. Jesus will say, "I took away their sins. They are not guilty. Heaven is their home." Then God will send all His people to heaven. But how long can we live with Jesus in heaven?

Right now we know of nothing that goes on forever. What television show do you like most? Are you disappointed when it's over? What is your favorite food? When it's all gone, you probably wish you had more. Is Christmas one of your favorite times? Mine, too. But it ends, and we must wait a long time for the next Christmas.

The good news about heaven is that it never ends. Jesus will be with us always. Heaven with Jesus will be even better than our favorite television show or food. It will go on and on and on and on and on and on and on and . . . well, you probably get the idea.

Can anyone take heaven away from us? No. Never. On Judgment Day, God will destroy all His enemies. That probably sounds frightening, too, but God wants to protect us.

We don't know when God will have Judgment Day. But we can look forward to it as eagerly as we look forward to our favorite programs on television. We'll have a happy party to celebrate our new life with Jesus. All Christians will be at that party, but best of all, in heaven we'll be right there with Jesus.

Prayer. Dear Jesus, help us look joyfully forward to Judgment Day. Please come soon. Amen.

Celebrate!

Sunday of the Fulfillment: Is. 51:4–6; Jude 20–25 or Rev. 1:4b–8; Mark 13:32–37 or John 18:33–37

Text. My righteousness draws near speedily, My salvation is on the way, and My arm will bring justice to the nations. The islands will look to Me and wait in hope for My arm. *Is. 51:5*

Teaching aid. A calendar showing at least the next 12 months.

Gospel nugget. Jesus will establish an everlasting kingdom, where He will live with His people forever.

Our calendar for this year has only the month of December left before we begin a brand new year (*show calendar*). Then in the new year we have January, February, March, April, May, June, July, August, September, October, November, and December before we start over again, God willing. (*Page through calendar.*)

To what days do you look forward? (*Encourage responses. If children are reluctant, ask birthdays. Demonstrate how many days, weeks, or months they must wait until their favorite day.*) When your favorite day ends, you have to wait another whole year—12 months, 52 weeks, 365 days—until that exciting day comes again.

What kind of days do you like the least? I really dislike days when I'm sick or when I have to do things I don't like to do. Wouldn't it be great if we had favorite days every day?

Someday every day will be our favorite day. We'll never be sick. We won't get into trouble because we'll only be able to do good. We'll always enjoy what we are doing, and we'll never get bored. Every day will be better than any birthday, Christmas Day, Fourth of July, or any other favorite day we've ever had. Wouldn't you look forward to a day like that?

Our first day in heaven with Jesus will be the greatest day ever. We won't need calendars like this (*toss calendar aside*) because the first day will never end. We won't need our watches or clocks because we won't think about time. The good times with Jesus won't be over at eight o'clock, ten o'clock, or even midnight. You won't ever have to go to bed, and you'll never even be tired!

What do you think you might like most about heaven? I think I'll enjoy being able to walk right up to Jesus and put my arm around Him. He'll probably put His arm around me, too. Can you imagine? We'll actually be able to trade hugs with Jesus!

God in His Word promises that it won't be too long until we can live in heaven. (*Read text.*) But right now we must wait for that day. What can we do while we wait? One thing we can do is thank Jesus for getting us ready for heaven. He had to suffer and die on the cross to take away our sins because only people without sins can live in heaven.

We can thank Jesus for telling us something about heaven. We can thank Him that we don't have to worry about being good enough to live with Him. He made us good enough when He died for our sins. He gave us faith so we can believe in Him.

Another thing we can do while we wait is tell others how special it is to live now with Jesus. We can tell others that Jesus promised to come back to earth, and we can tell them not to be afraid because Jesus died to save them.

Finally, we can live happy lives here on earth while we wait to join Jesus in heaven. God wants us to enjoy living here. He wants us to have moments like birthdays, Thanksgiving, and Christmas. And every time we celebrate we can also think about the day when our celebrations will never end.

Prayer. Come, Lord Jesus. We'll be Your guest when with heaven we are blessed. Amen.

Scripture Index

The messages in this book are based on portions of the Old Testament (first) lessons for Year B of the three-year lectionary cycle.

Genesis
2:18
3:15
22:18a
28:13–14

Exodus
16:15
20:3, 7–8, 12–17
24:11

Numbers
11:29
21:9

Deuteronomy
4:7
5:14a
6:3, 6, 8
6:4
18:18

Joshua
24:15

1 Samuel
3:9

2 Samuel
7:11, 16

1 Kings
17:14–15
19:8

2 Kings
2:9
5:13

Job
7:1
38:1–2

Proverbs
9:6

Isaiah
25:8–9
35:4–7a
40:5
42:6–7
43:25
45:22, 25
50:8
51:5
52:7
53:11
60:1–3
61:10
62:1–2
64:8

Jeremiah
11:18
23:4
31:9
31:34b

Lamentations
3:22–23

Ezekiel
2:3
17:24
37:14

Daniel
7:9–10, 13–14
12:1, 3

Hosea
2:19–20

Joel
2:13

Amos
5:14
7:15

Jonah
3:10

Zechariah
9:9

Acts
1:24a
3:15, 19–20
4:12
4:31
8:35
11:23